ADVANCED ORGANIC GARDENING

Rodale's Guides

Grow-It

ADVANCED ORGANIC GARDENING

by Anna Carr

Rodale Press, Emmaus, Pa.

Printed in the United States of America on recycled paper, containing a high percentage of de-inked fiber.

Art direction by Karen A. Schell

Book design by Joan Peckolick

Illustrations by Jean Seibert

Library of Congress Cataloging in Publication Data

Carr, Anna, 1955–
    Advanced organic gardening.

    (Rodale's grow-it guides)
    Bibliography: p.
    Includes index.
    1. Vegetable gardening. 2. Organic gardening. I. Title. II. Series.
SB324.3.C37   635'.0484   81-17825
ISBN 0-87857-384-4 paperback   AACR2

2 4 6 8 10 9 7 5 3 1 paperback

CONTENTS

INTRODUCTION/**1**

NEW APPROACHES TO SOIL PREPARATION/**4**

PLANNING FOR CONTINUOUS HARVESTS/**21**

VERTICAL GARDENING TO SAVE SPACE/**51**

IDEAS FOR ORGANIC FERTILIZING/**65**

NEW DEVELOPMENTS IN PEST CONTROL/**72**

EXTENDING THE GROWING SEASON/**88**

ADDING VARIETY TO THE VEGETABLE GARDEN/**102**

DESIGNING GARDEN EXPERIMENTS/**120**

SAVING YOUR OWN SEEDS/**125**

BIBLIOGRAPHY/**135**

INDEX/**137**

INTRODUCTION

T his book was written especially for gardeners who are familiar with basic gardening techniques and who are ready to expand their food-production skills and to try some different methods. It is full of ideas that we hope will inspire gardeners to explore more fully the potential of their gardens. Experimenting with new ways to grow food at home leads to a more productive garden and greater economic self-sufficiency, expands the range of foods you can enjoy cooking and eating and keeps gardening an enjoyable, exciting activity.

More and more people are discovering the special rewards of gardening these days. After a lull in the middle years of this century, gardening has returned as the number one national pastime. Vegetables far outnumbered flowers in America's 1980 gardens; over 30 million people grew vegetables with a fervor that hasn't been seen since we gardened for Victory in the 1940s.

The major motivation behind this surge is certainly economic. Vegetables aren't cheap. With the constant rise of fossil fuel and labor costs, they can only get still more dear. Growing our own lets us hold down most of these costs. It also lets us control the quality of the food we eat—to keep it fresher, more healthful and, most important, free from toxic chemicals. Pesticides, preservatives and dyes aren't listed on the pricing signs, so there's no telling what so-called "fresh" produce has been treated with by the time it reaches our grocer's shelves. At home, we can raise truly fresh crops without these added materials.

Important as these practical concerns are, there is still another incentive at work here, one so subtle that some gardeners might not recognize it themselves. This is nothing more than the simple pleasure of doing something ourselves—of turning the soil, planting seeds, cultivating, harvesting and, ultimately, being nourished by the fruits of our labors. Few things in this modern age are as satisfying—or mystifying—as this ancient cycle.

The recent boom in gardening has created a whole new range of techniques for raising food efficiently. A look to the past—the pre-mechanization years of food production—has led many gardeners to realize that the best gardens are not small farms but are rather special systems unique unto themselves. Gardening is its own science, with goals and methods quite different from those of the farm. Crops must be diversified, plantings intense and production long-term if the effort is going to be worthwhile. The gardener who grows plants in long, space-wasting rows with no thought to efficient use of soil, air and water will never achieve this level of productivity. Path areas must be carefully planned so as not to waste space; plantings must be mixed for insect control and soil improvement. Ancient Egyptian and Roman gardeners knew this. Nineteenth-century French market growers also knew it, and the Chinese have never forgotten it. By studying and testing some of their methods and adapting them to today's needs, we are learning how to get more out of our gardens without destroying the environment in the process.

Thus, the concepts of intensive and biodynamic gardening have come of age, and with them has come increased potential for gardeners to become self-sufficient in their food production. These techniques, together with recent developments in soil care, insect control, plant breeding, plant protectors and other areas, can help gardeners overcome the limitations of climate and growing space and raise more food than they ever thought possible.

At the Organic Gardening and Farming Research Center in Maxatawny, Pennsylvania, new ideas and methods are constantly being evaluated and compared. Scientists and technicians conduct controlled, carefully planned experiments to learn which of the "new" findings are really practical and useful in the home garden. Garden-related studies have involved topics ranging from insect-repellent crops to no-till planting to season-extending grow frames. In some cases, readers of Organic Gardening magazine have become involved in experiments through the Rodale Reader

Research Projects. Working in conjunction with the research center staff, these gardeners have tested the adaptability of crops to different growing conditions, the correct spacing of certain companion crops and the insect resistance of various crop varieties.

The important experimentation done at the Rodale's research center and at other institutions around the world is of little use unless gardeners put these findings into practice. Try thinking of your garden as not just a hobby but also as a kind of cottage industry that can be productive as well as enjoyable. Take the time to keep abreast of developments in this new science of gardening, and don't be afraid to try even the most unconventional techniques. You've nothing to lose and everything to gain. By expanding the range of crops you grow and experimenting with newer methods, perhaps even developing some new ones of your own, your interest in gardening will be well rewarded.

NEW APPROACHES TO SOIL PREPARATION

Horticultural research continues to support a principle that organic gardeners have affirmed for years: a garden is only as good as its soil. Organic matter, drainage, tilth and fertility are at the very heart of successful crop production. Working manure, compost and similar materials deeply into the soil enhances all of these elements and makes it possible for the ground to support a variety of healthy crops.

But good soil care doesn't end here. Studies by the United States Department of Agriculture (USDA) show that these practices are almost worthless if the ground becomes compacted. Unfortunately, compaction does not occur at the surface, where it could be easily loosened by spading. Instead, a hard layer forms 1 or 2 feet below ground level, just beneath the area you've tilled or spaded; finer cultivated soil particles press against the uncultivated subsoil, forming a compaction layer or plow pan. This layer, whether caused by foot traffic or heavy equipment, is impervious to roots and greatly limits moisture penetration and uptake.

Since vegetable plants may send roots 6 feet deep in ideal soils, the plow pan at a depth of 1 to 2 feet poses a serious limitation. Like a house plant growing in a container that's too small, the vegetable will slow its growth rate, reduce its productivity and possibly wilt. According to USDA scientist Dr. Albert Trouse, soil compaction can reduce a crop's efficiency from 25 to 50 percent, even if the pan isn't rock hard.

Soil compaction is a serious problem that can occur every time you step on your garden soil

Ironically, the better you cultivate the soil, the more susceptible it becomes to compaction. "A well-cultivated garden soil," explains Dr. Trouse, "may need as little as 3½ pounds of pressure per square inch to form a pan. People walking flat-footed create about 5½ pounds. When they get on their toes or heels, that goes up to 15 pounds, and you really have compaction." When you till or deeply spade the garden every spring and establish pathways that you walk on all summer long, you are creating a network of plow pans just below the depth of cultivation. As pathways are moved from year to year, the compaction layer extends and eventually runs under the entire garden. The deeper you cultivate the soil, the deeper and harder the plow pan becomes as long as you continue to walk on the soil.

How can you overcome the problem of compaction? This chapter will offer two solutions: growing beds and no-till strips.

Two ways to avoid soil compaction are to establish growing beds and permanent pathways or to plant in no-till strips

Making Growing Beds

Establishing growing beds and permanent, uncultivated access paths is a practice consistent with both the wisdom of ancient gardeners and the findings of modern research. Once you have created these beds, no one need ever walk on them again. Each is just 3 to 5 feet wide and allows you to plant, weed, cultivate and harvest by standing on the surrounding pathways. Over the years, these paths will become rock hard and impenetrable, while the growing beds will remain loose and rich.

These benefits, combined with increased yields from close planting (see the chart Comparative Yields: Single-Row and Intensive Bed Gardens) and more economical use of fertilizers and water, make growing beds the most efficient way for many gardeners to raise their vegetables. Planting in beds also makes it possible to apply water and organic enrichments only where they're needed, without wasting anything on walkways, as happens in conventional gardens. As long as soil has been deeply dug and enriched, crops may be planted close together, making possible yields that are two or three times those of a typical row garden.

COMPARATIVE YIELDS: SINGLE-ROW AND INTENSIVE BED GARDENS

Crop	Conventional Garden Average Yield (lbs./100 sq. ft.)	Growing Bed Average Yield (lbs./100 sq. ft.)
Beans, Bush	8.2	72
Broccoli	17.4	39
Carrots	58.9	150
Corn	15.3	34
Lettuce, Head	48.6	150
Lettuce, Leaf	48.6	202
Onions	68.6	200
Peppers, Green	18.8	83
Spinach	12.1	100
Tomatoes	30.7	194

To get the most benefit from a growing bed, choose a permanent location, deeply spade the soil and work in plenty of organic matter to establish a rich, loose growing medium

There are many ways to construct a growing bed, some more involved than others. Technically, a growing bed is nothing more than a section of your conventional garden used as a wide planting strip and undivided by paths. In most temperate regions, you will want to make beds slightly higher than the surrounding ground level so they warm up early in spring. If the native soil is very heavy, shallow or otherwise unsuitable, you may have to import good quality topsoil in order to build a deep enough growing bed. When this is the case, you must construct walls 1 to 3 feet high to keep the soil in place. For instructions, see the next section in this chapter, Building Beds with Structured Sides. If your soil is light and you live in a desert region, it's best to create the sunken bed or "pan," described in the section titled Pan Gardening and Trenching in Desert Soils, found later in this chapter.

In most cases, however, thorough spading along with the addition of compost and manure will turn native soil into an excellent growing medium. The real key to success is the digging, which must be deep but should not disturb existing soil strata. This method is called double-digging, or bastard trenching. Popularized in this country by the late Alan Chadwick, a horticulturist well known for his intensive gardening efforts, double-digging is the basis of successful bed gardening. It is particularly necessary in soils that are less than perfect to begin with, but it really should be used in all areas where you are striving for top yields. If you cannot easily insert a heavy metal rod 3 feet into the soil, then double-digging is a must. It will loosen the soil at all levels so roots and water can penetrate easily.

Before you actually begin the digging, use graph paper to map exactly where each growing bed should

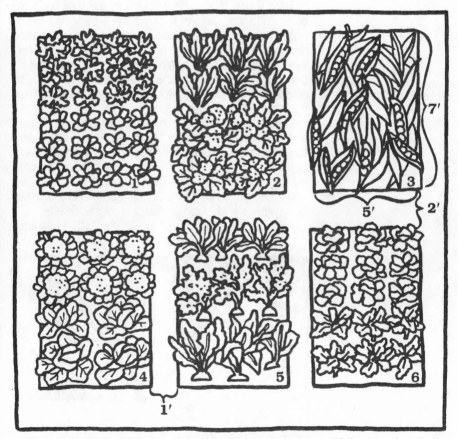

INTENSIVE BED DESIGN: *Growing beds are a very efficient and orderly way to use gardening space; they save you time, labor and fertilizer. Bed #1 contains looseleaf lettuce and spinach; bed #2 contains Swiss chard and broccoli; bed #3, peas; bed #4, cauliflower and cabbage; bed #5, radishes, carrots and beets; and bed #6, Bibb lettuce and mustard greens.*

be placed, marking its length and width. Remember to limit bed width to about 5 feet so that the center is easily accessible from each side. Paths may be as narrow as 1 foot, but your work will be easier if there's sufficient room for a wheelbarrow to pass and for you to reach into one bed without backing over the crops in the next. Arrange the entire system of beds and walkways in a pattern that is attractive and makes the most use of sunlight.

Like most good things, double-digging requires a lot of hard work. If you are working in soil that has not been cultivated before, it may take 5 to 15 hours to prepare a 5 by 20-foot bed. Converting an existing garden patch to beds will not take as long. No matter what kind of soil you begin with, the preparation will become much easier as the years go on. After a few seasons, you'll be able to renew each bed with a minimum of digging.

During your first year, however, try to start small, and begin preparations in fall so you'll have less work to do at spring planting time. Make just one or two beds in a new area of your yard, or convert a small part of your present garden to beds. In that way, you'll be able to compare conventional and intensive bed systems and judge performance for yourself.

Begin by marking off the bed area. With a spading

REMOVING SOD: *Cut along the outline of your plot with a spade or spading fork (left). Slip the spade under the sod about 1" below the surface; lift and roll back the grass. Continue this process, working across the bed in spade-wide strips.*

fork or a sharp, flat-edged shovel, cut straight down around the entire bed. If the area has not recently been cultivated, you'll need to remove the sod. Slip the shovel just under the sod, about 1 inch below the surface, and pull up to sever the roots. Roll back the grass, exposing the soil beneath. Continue working across the bed in spade-wide strips, rolling the sod and cutting it as it accumulates. When you've removed it all, chop it and add it to the compost heap, or cut it into sections for making turf loam, a rich potting mixture.

To make turf loam, layer pieces of sod with like sides together; place one section of sod on the ground, dirt side up, then another on top of it, grass side up.

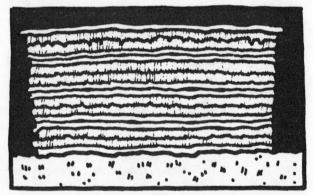

TURF LOAM: *A rich potting soil called turf loam can be made by stacking layers of sod, one on top of the other, and then leaving it to compost. Lay the pieces of sod with like sides together: grass to grass or dirt to dirt, building layers until you've used all the sod. Over the course of a year, the layers of sod will slowly decay and produce a wonderfully rich potting mix.*

Continue stacking pieces, dirt against dirt, or grass against grass. These piles will slowly decay, eventually forming a light, rich potting soil.

Some gardeners prefer to work the sod into the bed soil. Doing so may produce some weeds the first years, but this problem can be avoided if the pieces are small and are buried at various levels deep in the bed. Allow several months for decomposition to take place before fertilizing, shaping and planting the bed.

Sod can be buried in a newly dug bed or removed and stacked to make turf loam

Once you've removed the sod, you can begin double-digging. Across one end of the bed, dig a trench 2 feet wide and the depth of your spade, about 1 foot. Digging any deeper will bring the less fertile subsoil to the surface. Place the removed soil in a wheelbarrow, and set it aside for later use. Next, use your spading fork to loosen the subsoil at the bottom of the trench. Insert the fork as deeply as possible, and move the handle back and forth. Do not remove or turn the subsoil; just break it up. Your goal is to improve aeration and drainage.

When the bottom of your first trench has been completely subsoiled to a depth of about 24 inches, dig a second trench 2 feet wide and 1 foot deep, and use its soil to fill the first trench. Transfer the soil carefully, sliding each shovelful into the trench so that the layers aren't disturbed. You can mix organic fertilizers, sand and other soil conditioners into this topsoil or use them as partial replacement for a rather poor native soil. Hard-line double-diggers, however, prefer to add fertilizers afterward in a separate step. If you're short of time or energy, work in the necessary soil-builders as you go, but be sure to keep them in the top 6 to 8 inches of the bed, where they will be most helpful.

The trenching and subsoiling continue the entire length of the bed. Since newly spaded areas need never be stepped upon, the soil should remain light and slightly raised above the surrounding ground level. When the last trench has been subsoiled, fill it with the earth removed from the first trench you dug.

Let the bed rest before continuing to work on it. Heavy soils can be left all winter in this state and will actually benefit most from frost heavage when the surface is roughest. If your soil is sandy, you should rake and smooth it a bit if it is to sit all winter. If you are digging the beds in spring, just water them gently and let them rest for at least two days.

At this point, you may work in soil conditioners and fertilizers if you have not already done so. Keep conditioners in the upper strata, but do not leave rich manure on the surface, or it will dry out. Because of the number of crops the bed will be supporting, the soil should be rich and have a high content of organic matter. This does not mean that you should add any more fertilizers to beds than you would to your con-

Rely on lots of slow-release organic materials such as aged manure or compost as your basic soil amendments

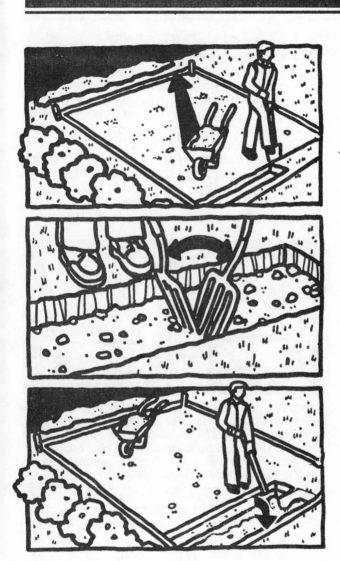

DOUBLE-DIGGING: *Dig a trench along one end of the garden, put the soil in a wheelbarrow and transfer it to the other end of the garden, outside the perimeter. Loosen the soil in the bottom of the trench with a spading fork. Dig a second trench next to the first one, shoveling the soil from it to the first trench. Do the same across the entire garden, filling the last trench with the soil that was removed from the first trench. This is by far the best way to loosen the soil in your garden.*

ventional garden. Overfertilization and its related problems can occur here as anywhere. Apply bone meal, rock phosphate, wood ashes and other substances based on your own knowledge of the soil and the results of soil tests. You'll find that fertilizers and mulches go a long way since none of them end up on path areas.

Once you've added fertilizers, it's time to shape the growing bed. Depending on soil conditions, beds are mounded or flat-topped, with a base about 1 foot wider than the upper surface. In a mounded bed, the top is dome shaped, with the sides evenly sloping down to surrounding paths. Plant sides as well as top with crops.

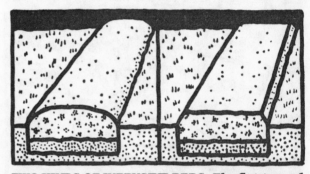

TWO KINDS OF INTENSIVE BEDS: *The flat-topped bed on the right is best for heavy soils or for first-year beds. The mounded bed on the left is more productive, because you can plant the sides as well as the top, but is best to use when your soil is rich, loose and humusy.*

In a flat-topped bed, plants are grown only on the level top because the sides are too steep. A drainage ditch around the base of the bed, or a ridge outlining the top, helps divert rainwater away from paths and into the beds. This shape is good for heavy soil, easily eroded soil or for any first-year bed that does not have a high humus content. After you have cultivated the ground for several seasons, you may be able to use the more productive mound design.

After the initial preparation year, growing beds need very little digging. In the fall, remove garden refuse, and mulch or plant a green manure crop. In spring, work in additional manure, compost, bone meal, lime and other necessary amendments, and spade the top

12 to 24 inches of soil. If drainage problems persist, it may be necessary to double-dig every two or three years. Since you will probably need to step into the bed to double-dig it, the disadvantages almost outweigh the benefits. You may be better off simply building higher beds by adding more topsoil and constructing structured sides.

Building Beds with Structured Sides

Where native soil is very poor, or where terracing is necessary to accommodate a slope, it is sometimes necessary to construct slightly higher growing beds. These may be 1 to 3 feet high with sides built of wood, stone, adobe or cement. If your topsoil is very shallow (perhaps in a newly developed area), if the water table is high or if the ground is simply rocky, beds with structured sides are one of the best techniques you can choose. They are neat, attractive and easy to maintain. Like the standard growing beds, they warm up early in spring and remain well drained. The only problems they present are the slugs, snails and insects that like to hide in the walls. However, bugs are usually only a minor problem if the soil is light and if the beds are situated in a sunny location.

Unless you plan on adding 2 or 3 feet of soil, begin by double-digging the bed area. The digging will give crops maximum drainage and is advisable even if the growing beds are going to be quite high. Where heavy clay soil causes severe drainage problems, remove the native soil to a depth of 1 or 2 feet and replace it with sandy loam or a gravelly medium. To correct a high water table, install tile drains or build gravel-filled drainage trenches. Since materials and techniques differ from site to site, consult your county agent or soil conservationist for help with this kind of problem. Single-digging to a depth of 1 foot is sometimes sufficient for the structured bed. For best production, remember that you should have about 3 feet of loose, well-drained soil.

The materials you select for constructing the sides of the growing beds should be attractive and long lasting. Railroad ties stacked two or three high have both qualities. They are also hard to move, expensive and, if freshly creosoted, possibly toxic to plants. If you have your heart set on railroad ties, look for used

If you can push a rod 3 feet into the soil without encountering any barriers, then single-digging is sufficient preparation for the beds

ones; they'll be cheaper and won't leach toxic creosote. Stacked or mortared cement blocks are also stable and sturdy when steel supporting rods are used to keep them in place. For the ambitious, adobe walls or mortared stone walls are permanent and beautiful.

Probably the simplest and most space-saving framing material is lumber. Rough redwood planks, unstreaked and pure in color, will last about 20 years, with cheaper grades rotting a bit sooner. Tight-knot cedar is equally attractive and long lasting. But both redwood and cedar are expensive.

If you want to use railroad ties to make sides for raised beds, you must find used ties, or let ties freshly water-proofed with cre-osote sit outdoors until some of the creosote leaches out. Creosote is toxic to plants

STRUCTURED-SIDE BEDS: *Beds with structured sides are attractive and will last for years. Vertical stakes support redwood planks that form the sides of the bed shown here.*

The least expensive option is to buy untreated or pressure-treated lumber and coat it yourself with a nontoxic wood preservative like copper naphthenate. Purchase 1- to 2-inch-thick boards for the most durability. Use them singly, or one above the other for a higher bed. Nail them to sharpened vertical supports for extra strength and anchoring to the ground.

Some gardeners line the bottom of each bed with chicken wire or screening in order to keep out moles and groundhogs. But unless the screen is placed 2 or more feet below the surface and consists of mesh that is ¼ inch or larger, it could interfere with rooting or even drainage. As an alternative, make a vertical screen barrier around the bed, just under the sides. It will create an underground fence and keep out all but the most persistent rodents.

To fill the bed structure, use a rich combination of topsoil, organic matter, sand (if native soil is high in clay) and other substances. By removing topsoil from surrounding paths, you can reduce the amount of earth that must be hauled in from long distances. This imported soil, plus the soil already in the bed and manure or compost, will be sufficient to fill the structure.

After you've added fertilizer and thoroughly mixed the soil, allow the raised bed to rest for several days. You may find that you need to add more material after the soil has settled. Shape the bed in the mounded or flat-topped design, or level the soil at the height of the bed sides. The latter shape yields a bit less growing area, but it is better in dry areas, where structured sides will help reduce moisture evaporation.

Raised beds allow excess moisture to drain off from wet, heavy soils, while sunken beds conserve precious moisture where soil is porous and the climate is dry

Pan Gardening and Trenching in Desert Soils

Several Organic Gardening magazine readers have adapted the raised bed concept to fit the special needs of desert soil and severe drought conditions. Where rainfall is minimal, raised beds with or without structured sides tend to be somewhat impractical: soil raised above the surrounding ground level becomes too hot; precious moisture evaporates in the intense sunlight; the ground is left open to damaging winds. Even if the soil is quite shallow because of hardpan, raised beds do not usually work unless extensive irrigation is possible.

What does work is a kind of sunken growing bed known as a "pan." With paths raised some 12 inches above fertile growing beds, planting soil stays relatively cool and moist.

To construct pans, begin by spading the soil in a 3- to 5-foot-wide bed area. Remove and set aside the topsoil. Poke holes through any hardpan with a rod or spading fork, and remove rocks. Remove some of the very poor subsoil and place it in path areas so that you have more room in the sunken beds for rich soil and organic matter. Mix topsoil with water-holding organic matter, and use this mixture to fill the pans. Finished pans should be about 6 inches below the access paths. Building a dike around each pan, about 12 inches on all sides, will further protect the growing areas and direct rainfall into them.

PAN GARDEN FOR DESERT AREAS: *In dry desert soil, gardening in beds sunk below ground level helps conserve every bit of moisture and channel it to plant roots.*

Over the years, sunken beds will become rich and moist, and the hard walkways between them will become so impenetrable to moisture that water will flow down the dikes into the growing areas

For best results and for most efficient use of organic soil-builders, keep these pans permanent. Use center walkways for weeding and watering, and mulch the pans as seedlings become established. In fall, apply compost or other material to the bottom of each pan.

Dry, crusty soils also benefit from trenching, a technique that can be used in conjunction with pan gardening, conventional rowed gardens or intensive beds. Use it in isolated spots for individual hills of vine crops or for beds of other water-loving vegetables. Its only drawback is that large quantities of straw-rich stable manure are needed, which can be inaccessible or too expensive for gardeners.

To construct a trench, or trenched bed, for all or some of your crops, begin by marking off bed areas or pans about 3 feet wide. Remove 1 foot of soil from the bed areas, and set the soil aside for later use. In the bottom of the bed, dig a trench about 2 feet deep and 1 foot wide. Fill this trench with fresh, coarse stable litter, packing and tamping it so that the material is quite dense. This will serve as a wick, drawing up moisture from the soil below. Next, mix the soil you removed from the bed with one part well-rotted manure and two parts peat, sand or other materials that will build texture. Use this mixture to fill the bed, hilling up the center in a mound shape. Water the soil thoroughly and deeply, and allow it to settle for several days before

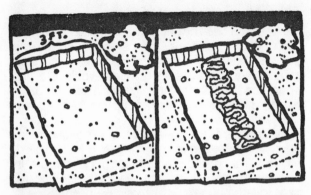

TRENCHING: *Remove 1 foot of soil from a 3-foot-wide bed, and pile the soil next to the bed. In the bottom of the 1-foot-deep bed, dig a trench 1 foot wide and 2 feet deep and fill it with stable litter. This acts as a wick to draw up moisture from deep in the soil.*

planting. When the ground is dry enough to work, you may proceed as with any garden bed.

Benefits of a trenched garden will extend beyond the first season. In the fall, the area may be deeply spaded so that the manure is worked into the soil at all levels. Often, one year of trenching improves the soil's water-holding capacity so much that standard double-digging and the addition of organic matter are sufficient soil preparation in future years. Otherwise, you will need to remove 1 foot of soil every spring, dig and fill the trench with manure and replace the soil before planting again. At any rate, try to keep the beds permanent to prevent compaction.

No-Till Gardening: Growing Vegetables in Living Sod

The idea of planting crops directly in your lawn is unconventional, but it's a technique that is proving itself at the Organic Gardening and Farming Research Center and in the home gardens of several Rodale employees. It requires little work other than occasional mowings and has untold benefits for the soil. Crops themselves seem to benefit from their competition with the sod by developing deeper roots and often yielding more per plant than crops grown in conventional tilled plots. Soil remains uncompacted and water retention and drainage are excellent, even in relatively poor soil that has never been heavily fertilized or tilled. Pans have no chance to form since you neither spade nor plow the ground. As long as you mow the sod between planting strips, weeds are unable to set seed. Problems of soil erosion and runoff are virtually eliminated, probably making this technique the best option for steep hillside gardens.

The only problems that may occur in no-till gardening, or vegetable-sod interplanting, as it is also called, involve selection of crops and mulching materials. In experiments over the past few years, tomatoes, beans, corn, squash and various greens have been tested in no-till strips. Not only did these crops require less maintenance, but some of them even produced better than tilled plantings.

Whether peas, peppers, melons and other crops will perform as well in competition with sod remains to be seen. It seems likely that root crops, so dependent on a loose growing medium, will not do as well as the crops tested so far.

Researchers have found several workable mulching materials to use on the no-till strips. Black plastic sheeting, a biodegradable type sold as Ecolite, does an excellent job of reducing weed growth, and it warms the soil during cold, wet weather. Chopped green alfalfa, applied 6 inches deep, does not warm the soil as thoroughly in the spring but performs better overall. During dry weather, chopped alfalfa conserves moisture more effectively than the plastic and, as it decomposes, it provides crops with additional nitrogen. Other organic mulches, such as grass clippings, newspaper and compost, are also suggested by the Rodale experimenters.

To establish a no-till vegetable garden in your lawn, mark off growing strips 8 to 20 inches wide with paths between that are sufficiently wide for your lawn mower to pass. On a large scale, you may wish to till the narrow planting strip for quicker seeding, but it is unnecessary in the small home garden. The mulch you apply to the strip will loosen the soil so that digging is not needed. Simply lay the plastic sheeting or organic material over the planting strip and allow it to sit undisturbed for about a week. During this time, existing sod will begin to lose its vigor and break down.

When you are ready to plant, cut a slit in the plastic

Mulching a week before planting in a no-till strip will loosen the soil and cause the sod to start breaking down

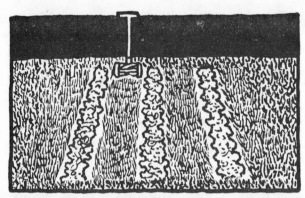

NO-TILL GARDENING: *Mark off planting strips in the lawn, placing them far enough apart so a lawn mower can pass between them. Mulch the planting strips. A week later pull back the mulch and plant.*

mulch or make a "pocket" in the organic mulch where each seed or seedling is to be set. Scratch away the sod surface, plant and replace the soil and mulch. If the strip has been tilled, then plant seeds and seedlings in the usual fashion.

Make plantings in single rows or in a series of staggered rows, depending on the width of the growing strip. Follow standard spacing recommendations for between-plant distances as given on seed packets. The intensive planting distances supplied in this book should not be used in a new "lawn" garden, since these are only for use in deeply spaded growing beds.

Throughout the season, add more organic mulch as needed to keep down weeds and maintain a moist environment for crop roots. If you wish to side-dress crops, simply pull back the mulch and apply the dried blood, manure or other material alongside the growing strip. You'll find that by midsummer sod will have all but disappeared around the growing plants.

Periodically mow the path areas, and save clippings to use as additional mulch on the strips. You'll be able to walk or work in the garden anytime, even after a rain, if the grass is providing a thick cushion. At the end of the season, mulch the growing strips, adding any necessary slow-release fertilizers, or plant a green manure winter cover crop for tilling under the following spring.

After the first two or three years of vegetable produc-

As long as you keep the paths well mowed they will remain protected from compaction as people walk on them, and weeds will be no problem

tion, rotate the strips. Plant a mixture of short white clover and bluegrass in the growing strips, and plant vegetables in the old "path" areas you have been mowing. Because the sod cover has been maintained, these walkways should be excellent growing strips. The clover strips will become your pathways for one or two years, after which they will once again be growing strips while the old paths are planted in clover. White clover is far superior to lawn grass for sod interplanting. It contributes nitrogen and loosens the soil. In combination with bluegrass, it forms a dense, hardy ground cover that won't die out as you tramp across it. In fact, short white clover is so beneficial to the soil and presents such minimal competition for vegetable crops that you may wish to start no-till gardening in your conventional, tilled garden. Plant short white clover in the path areas in mid-August or spring, keep it well mowed, and allow it to grow right up around mulched seedlings. You will find there is less need for expensive mulching materials, much less soil compaction and the added benefit of "free" soil nutrients.

PLANNING FOR CONTINUOUS HARVESTS

Ever find yourself with too much of one vegetable and not enough of another? With all crops picked by July 15 and no more to harvest until the end of the month? Or with two weeks remaining in the growing season and your garden already finished producing? These dilemmas result from poor garden planning.

Eager to get things rolling in the spring, we plant the entire garden with little or no thought to how long crops will occupy their growing spaces and how best to keep those spaces in continuous production. Lettuce is sown in the lettuce row, corn in the corn row, squash in the squash row. Subsequent plantings, if they are made at all, come only after entire sections have been cleared of crops. Thus, the garden produces "one-shot" harvests. All the corn ripens at once. Lettuce and carrots are prolific for three weeks. Squash zooms into production for several weeks before borers get the better of it. Before and after these crescendos of productivity, there are long periods when most crops are in their seed and seedling stages. Not only is there nothing to pick during these times, but because the young plants use only a part of their allotted growing areas, a great deal of light, water and soil go unused.

In the most efficient organic gardens the story is quite different. Intensive planting and timing schemes, along with thorough soil management, produce double or triple yields. Quick-growing perishables like lettuce and

Even the smallest garden can be managed so that no space is wasted and bounteous harvests are evenly distributed over the entire growing season

21

radishes are kept in constant, fresh supply, providing just what the family needs when it needs it. Pickling cucumbers, tomatoes, beans, corn, squash and other crops for canning and freezing as well as fresh eating ripen at regular intervals and in manageable amounts. From the last spring frost to the first fall one and beyond, the garden offers a daily assortment of ripe, fresh-for-the-picking vegetables. There are still great spurts of production as certain crops reach their peak, but these are planned so the gardener knows when to expect them.

This kind of harvest is easiest to create in intensive growing beds, where double-digging and added organic matter create optimum conditions. But excellent results are also possible from the no-till "lawn" garden, the desert pan and even the conventional rowed vegetable patch. Success requires careful long-range planning and daily attention. Design and timing must be planned in a way slightly more mathematical than some of us are used to. However, as food prices continue to rise, the significantly higher yields and improved quality resulting from more detailed planning will begin to look very good indeed.

The importance of good garden planning can't be overstressed. Careful planning and management will maximize the economic benefits of any vegetable garden

Choose Early and Late Varieties

One easy way to extend and stagger harvests of specific vegetables is to plant several different varieties of a crop, each with a different rate of maturity. Most seed companies sell early and late cabbage, for example, with estimated days to maturity ranging from just 55 days to 105. If you plant several varieties simultaneously, some cabbage will be ready in just 55 days, then again one or two weeks later, and again even later in the season. Other crops with several varieties that mature at different rates include corn, lettuce, squash and (now that a subarctic variety has been developed) even tomatoes. Be sure to select only those varieties suited to your climate, soil and general garden conditions; also consider each variety's taste and quality as well as maturity rate.

Successions and Relays

To further distribute harvests and make maximum use of garden space, you can practice succession and relay planting. With these systems, you can juggle planting and picking so that the soil is kept in constant production and steady harvests are assured.

To practice succession planting, replace short-season vegetables like lettuce, spinach, snap beans, turnips and sweet corn with new crops as soon as they are harvested. For example, you could replace early beans with more beans, or with carrots or lettuce. Squash could follow cabbage; corn could follow peas. Although most gardeners practice a kind of haphazard succession planting, few plan their cropping order to take full advantage of the season and garden space.

To employ relay planting, plant a second crop in the garden even before the early one is harvested. Sow seeds of a given crop every one to three weeks so that harvests continue uninterrupted over a long period. To achieve a kind of timed interplanting, plant relays between already established initial plantings. This makes it possible to produce still more vegetables from a given piece of land. Choose crops that need only a small amount of space during early growth, and tuck them in among another growing crop. The partial shade and moist environment are beneficial to most germinating seeds and young seedlings. By the time the relay crop is in need of more space, the initial crop will have been harvested. In this way, spring cauliflower plantings might be interplanted with endive seedlings set out just three weeks before harvest. The young endive will reach their peak growth just as the cauliflower is being picked. In order to have success with mixed relays, however, you need to be fully acquainted with interplanting techniques. For a complete discussion of mixed plantings, read the Interplanting section of this chapter. Here, in this section, we will cover just the basics of timing and crop selection.

In the South, where the growing season is long, possibilities for successions and relays are almost endless. Set out cabbage in March, with tomato relays planted alongside in early April. By July, tomatoes will have been harvested, and broccoli can be set out, with turnips or carrots ending the season in October.

Such luxuriously long, frost-safe periods are rare north of Louisiana, however, and in most temperate parts of the U.S. and Canada very careful planning is needed to squeeze in as many crops as possible between last spring and first fall frosts. The choice of succession

Succession planting is following one crop with another; relay planting is interplanting the second crop before the first crop is harvested

and relay crops is limited by the vegetables' required days to maturity, their preferred temperatures and the length of your area's growing season. Follow the information concerning days to maturity found on the back of seed packets. To plan late summer or fall successions and relays, count backwards from your area's predicted first fall frost. If you don't mind taking a small chance on the weather (and what gardener doesn't), then use a date of two weeks after the first frost to mark the "end" of your growing season. Cloches, row covers, mulching and other protective devices can usually extend the season at least two weeks, and even up to six weeks for some crops. A number of very hardy vegetables, including the Chinese brassicas, kale and certain root crops, actually benefit from quite cold temperatures and may be planted fairly late in the summer.

If you use transplants instead of seed sown directly, a greater number of successions and relays will be possible. This is particularly true of crops like lettuce, cole crops, onions and others which respond well to transplanting. Remember that starting transplants is not just an early spring occupation. It should carry right on into late summer or fall. Many gardeners use an uncovered cold frame or an outdoor planting bench for just this purpose. Soil can be tailored to the needs of germinating seeds and young plants. In a relatively small area, you can raise many seedlings for later use in the garden while the garden itself is being used for productive crops. While tomato seedlings are growing in the "nursery," you can sow an entire crop of leaf lettuce between the cabbage plants. By the time you've picked the cabbage, lettuce is ready to thin, and the tender leaves are all set for a salad. Set the tomato plants in the row as lettuce finishes its growth. As long as seedlings are properly hardened off and are given adequate protection from sun and wind during the first few days in the garden, they will suffer little setback.

Continuous harvests and high yields are not the only advantages of relays and successions. Since growing beds or rows support a diversity of crops at various stages of development, pest and disease problems rarely occur. Successions and relays may even be a kind of crop insurance, replacing any plants which do become infested. Squash planted in spring may be infested with

Seed companies base estimations of days to maturity on spring plantings; midsummer sowings will mature much more rapidly since the ground and air are already warm

borers by early summer. However, if you're practicing relay planting, there will be other unaffected plants to take over production. Often, seed sown just one or two weeks later will have missed the egg-laying period that devastates an early crop. See the Insect Emergence Times chart in the chapter New Developments in Pest Control, found later in this book, for more information on staggering relays to avoid certain pest problems.

Where possible, second and third crops in an area should be in entirely different families from previous crops grown there. This precaution will eliminate many potential insect and disease problems before they begin. Follow snap beans not just with other beans but with carrots or lettuce as well. Follow cabbage with tomatoes, not broccoli. Research indicates that nematode populations, for one, tend to build up when the same crop is grown over and over in the same place. Different crops attract different types of nematodes and, by the same token, different insect pests and beneficials as well. So, by all accounts, it's a good idea to use successions and relays as opportunities for mixed cropping and as a sort of short-term rotation. Your garden will be the healthier for it in the long run.

To discourage pests like nematodes, succession and relay crops should be of different botanical families from the crops they follow

One other benefit of diversified successions and relays is improved garden soil. Thorough fall and spring soil preparations should make the soil rich in organic matter and available nutrients. Use the time between successional sowings to work in compost or well-rotted manure.

During the first year of gardening in a spot, it may be best to plant entire patches with "proximity" crops — vegetables that are sown or planted simultaneously and mature at about the same time. This practice makes it easier to clear the area periodically and to loosen and enrich the soil thoroughly. Suitable proximity crops include spring onions, carrots, radishes, early lettuce and spinach sown as a group; tender, long-season crops like tomatoes, peppers and late sweet corn; and late season crops like leeks, celeriac, kohlrabi, spinach and brussels sprouts (transplants).

For further improvements, plan successions and relays according to each vegetable's nutrient needs and the benefits it brings to the soil. You can then arrange the successions so that no single nutrient is depleted and the ground is actually enriched. Follow heavy nitrogen

Plans can always be changed if crops fail and different successions are necessary, but having a master plan on paper will force you to be efficient and thorough in your use of garden space

feeders, such as corn, lettuce or cucumbers, with legumes, which replace part of the lost nutrient, or with root crops, which, almost by definition, need little nitrogen.

Since root crops do a fine job of loosening the soil, follow them with shallow-rooted leaf crops such as lettuce, spinach, peas or beans. Where heavier feeders are to be followed by other heavy-feeding crops, be sure to work in plenty of well-rotted manure, compost or other organic material as the second crop is being planted. Although it may take several weeks for the material to break down, it will eventually improve the soil and replenish lost elements. For the well-balanced, well-timed garden, build successions and relays with long- and short-term crops, always keeping in mind potential pest and nutrient problems. Plan second and third crops early in the season so you know what soil amendments are required and can estimate final harvest quantities of each crop.

Among the very fast-growing vegetables that grow from seed to maturity in 60 days or less and can be quickly replaced by succession crops are beets, snap beans, wax beans, early corn, garden cress, kohlrabi, lettuce, green onions, Chinese mustard, radishes, spinach and turnips. Fast-growing transplants include early cole crops, celery, collards and endive. You can plant quick-in, quick-out crops every two or three weeks throughout much of the growing season, depending on climate. They are also useful as "catch-crops" that precede or follow other mid- and late-season vegetables.

Vegetables that need slightly more time to mature include midseason cabbage, cauliflower, Chinese cabbage, broccoli, carrots and corn. Use them in relays or successions with longer or shorter term crops.

Vegetables that provide a long harvest period and remain in the garden for most of the season, but not usually all of it, include cucumbers, pole beans, soybeans, peppers, leeks, New Zealand spinach, summer squash and tomatoes. These crops often make good second plantings to follow very quick early spring crops such as greens or transplanted early cabbage. You can also follow them with short-season relays in the fall.

Vegetables that need all season to mature, usually occupying the garden from the last spring frost to mid-fall, include various beans grown for drying, full-

SHORT-SEASON CROPS FOR
SUCCESSION PLANTING

Crop	Days to Maturity	Season
Beets	50–60	Early or late
Garden Cress	10–20	Early or late
Kohlrabi	45–55	Early or late
Lettuce, Loose Head (and most leaf types)	55–70	Early or late
Lettuce, Oak Leaf (and other heat-resistant types)	45–60	Any
Onions, Green (from sets)	30–40	Any
Radishes	20–25	Any
Roquette	45	Early
Spinach	45–50	Early or late
Spinach, New Zealand	55	Midseason
Swiss Chard	55–60	Any
Turnips	40–75	Early or late

size carrots, winter cabbage, celeriac, brussels sprouts, eggplants, melons, peanuts, parsnips, pumpkins and winter squash. Although interplanting may be possible with these crops, successions are usually not practical in temperate areas.

Growing Degree-Days for Timing Vegetable Harvests
Gardeners who want to plan sweet corn harvests to

within several days can time relay plantings with the help of a simple mathematical formula. This technique, used by truck farmers who want to assure continued harvests throughout the season, requires some background information from your local weather bureau or your own garden records, as well as a few calculations. If you operate a roadside vegetable stand or just want to plan harvests around a vacation, the procedure is well worth the time it takes.

In order to grow and mature, vegetable plants need an extended amount of time when temperatures are warm. For some crops, such as potatoes, temperatures must be at least 45°F for growth and development to occur. Others, including most summer annual vegetables, need at least 50°F. This minimum temperature for growth is called the "base" or "threshold" temperature. (See the Base Temperatures for Vegetable Crops chart.)

BASE TEMPERATURES FOR VEGETABLE CROPS

The base temperature is the minimum temperature at which good growth occurs.

Temperature	Crops
40°F	Beets, broccoli, brussels sprouts, cabbage, horseradish, kale, kohlrabi, parsnips, radishes, spinach, Swiss chard, turnips
45°F	Artichokes, carrots, cauliflower, celeriac, celery, endive, Florence fennel, lettuce, parsley, peas, potatoes
50°F	Beans, corn, New Zealand spinach, squash
60°F	Cucumbers, eggplant, melons, peppers, sweet potatoes, tomatoes

Every day the mean temperature exceeds this base, a number of "heat units," or "growing degree-days," are said to be accumulated. Thus, the day's average temperature, minus the crop's base temperature, gives the number of heat units in that day. Unless temperatures become so hot that growth is actually hindered, the more heat units a crop acquires in a day, the faster growth occurs. These heat units are cumulative so that 20 units on Monday plus 18 on Tuesday and 23 on Wednesday result in a total of 61 growing degree-days in just three calendar days.

As an example we'll look at corn, which has a base temperature of 50°F and must accumulate 1,500 to 2,300 degree-days from seedling to harvest. To determine planting dates with this information, use last year's weather records to determine daily heat units. If you have kept garden records, the average over several years will be even more helpful. Since you won't be planting corn until after the first spring frost, you'll only need to figure heat units from this date to the first fall frost. Next, decide on a projected harvest date and count backward on the calendar, adding estimated degree-days until you have accumulated the necessary 1,500 for early varieties to 2,300 for late ones. This will give you the calendar planting date. Only after you have grown the same variety for several years will you know exactly how many degree-days it requires. This system will show that, although plantings may be made one week apart, harvests will not necessarily occur one week after another. Warmer temperatures could speed the second planting into production as much as several days behind the first one. Corn planted very early, before mean temperatures are well above 50°F, will not achieve much growth until the soil and air are warmer.

Interplanting

Interplanting (also called intercropping) is the term given to the practice of growing two or more crops in a given area at one time. It is a valuable space-saving technique in small gardens and, as long as it is not overdone, can increase the land's total harvest.

Although interplanting is just beginning to be accepted by American farmers, it has long been successfully practiced by oriental farmers and by gardeners around the world. Archaeological records indicate that ancient growers in the Americas, Asia and Europe practiced intercropping; there are written accounts to prove that the technique was widely used from the time of Christ to the nineteenth century. French market gardeners

On a farm scale, research has shown that fields planted to the highest yielding density for one crop can still be outproduced by fields where different crops are interplanted among the main one

29

refined the system in the eighteenth and nineteenth centuries as the basis of their intensive gardens, but soon afterward the practice fell into disuse. With the advent of motorized agricultural equipment, interplanting, along with bed planting and close, high-yield planting arrangements, was discontinued on farms and in gardens. With our present need to conserve energy and boost yields, interplanting is returning as a seemingly "new" concept in gardening and farming.

Interplanting is an excellent way to save space and can also improve yields and quality of crops

Advantages of interplanting are much touted in today's garden magazines, and rightly so. Once the basic needs of crops are understood, interplanting can be used not only to increase yields but to improve their quality as well. This is especially true in a raised bed where the soil has been deeply prepared and enriched with organic matter and close spacing patterns have been employed. Since plantings are mixed, and since each crop makes slightly different nutrient demands on the soil, fertility problems are practically nonexistent. Well-planned combinations also discourage the pests and diseases that are most damaging in single-cropped areas.

The key to successful interplanting is to know which crops grow well together and how they should be planted. Not only is timing a factor, as it is in any relays or successions, but so are plant shapes and sizes and their light and soil needs. Think of crops not as simple X shapes on a garden plan but as growing, three-dimensional plants with a complex series of needs.

Although planning an interplanted garden may seem an impossible task, finding planting combinations that are mutually beneficial to all crops is not really that difficult. Begin by looking at obvious pairings, based on the shapes and sizes of plants. Check to be sure that the crops share similar soil and nutrient needs. Finally, determine whether each crop would receive adequate light if grown fairly close to its companion. If you consider each factor and rule out combinations one by one, you will soon come up with a long list of effective interplantings for your garden.

Shapes and Sizes of Growing Plants: The varying shapes of vegetable crops, from the sprawling cucumber to the compact carrot, are the bane of the traditional gardener's existence. Too many plants just won't stay in the neat, orderly arrangement that has been mapped out on paper. They lean into the paths and shade neighboring crops that need sun. To avoid such problems, most conventional garden plans suggest large spacings between crops and rows. The result is wasted, unplanted and unused areas during most of the garden season.

In the interplanted, intensive garden, the diversity of crop shapes and sizes is put to good use. By allowing for shape in the overall plan, spacing, as discussed later in this chapter, can be quite close. Plan to tuck small, compact crops like radishes or onions beside larger bean or broccoli plants. Place plants with deep roots near shallow-rooted ones like cucumbers. The deep roots will feed far below the shallower rooting zone so that water and nutrient use is distributed over all soil levels. Interplant tall crops such as sweet corn with low, vining crops such as squash and cucumbers. Tomatoes, squash and similar climbing and vining vegetables can

INTERPLANTING FOR SHAPES AND SIZES OF PLANTS: *Interplanting can be used to take advantage of sizes and shapes of plants. This bed has trellised cucumbers at the north end, with head lettuce and onions intercropped.*

be staked or trained on trellises so that low plants can be grown nearby (see the next chapter, Vertical Gardening to Save Space, for more information).

Light Needs: Although most vegetable crops prefer full sunlight, some do quite well in partial shade during all or part of their life cycle. A few, including lettuce and

INTERPLANTING AND LIGHT NEEDS: Save space by interplanting crops according to their need for light. Tall-growing sun-lovers like tomatoes can be interplanted with crops like celery and leaf lettuce, which are shorter and need less light.

When planning interplantings, consider plant sizes and shapes and their needs for light and nutrients

other salad greens, actually prefer a cool, partially shady location to an open, sunny one. In midsummer, when soil and air temperatures are usually too high for broccoli, spinach and cabbage, these crops will flourish in a partly shaded spot, where temperatures will naturally be much lower than elsewhere.

As you interplant crops according to their shapes and sizes, be sure to accommodate their light needs as well. Keep light competition at a minimum. Make an asset out of the shade produced by trees, fences, buildings or neighboring vegetables. Keep tall plants to the north of light-loving shorter ones, and select shade-loving crops for those areas where sunlight is diffused.

Carrots, celery, cresses and most of the leaf crops are the best choices for interplanting with tall, shade-producing crops like tomatoes, beans and peppers. In midsummer, add to the list cool-season crops, like members of the cabbage family. Take care to give all these low-growing interplantings sufficient moisture, air and at least some light. No plant will grow without these essentials, even if the soil is quite rich.

Some tall-growing crops have so few leaves that they do not actually shade the surrounding area. Others have leaves angled upward so that no canopy forms. Corn, kohlrabi and sunflowers all offer many possibilities for interplanting with shorter crops needing light. Corn fares well with cucumbers, melons, squash or pumpkins as long as adequate space is allowed. You also can grow corn with bush beans, carrots, onions and almost any other crop that otherwise complements it in terms of nutrient needs and shape. Kohlrabi and sunflowers do well with beets, turnips, onions, cucumbers, squash, spinach or melons as interplanted relays or full-season crops.

Mulching with white plastic sheeting, aluminum foil, white gravel and other light-colored materials can increase yields of sun - loving crops like corn and tomatoes

If you don't think your crops are getting sufficient light, you can increase the amount they receive by mulching with a reflective material like aluminum foil. Of course, some light must be present in order for the mulch to have any effect. If spacing is too close or light is otherwise entirely restricted from the area, not even a good mulch will improve the situation.

The most important advice to remember about interplanting is to plan it carefully. Read seed catalogs for information on plant heights and choose shorter varieties for most interplanting situations. If you are in doubt about the effect that a crop will have on available light, don't establish a permanent interplanting with it. Leave a bit more space between rows or plants and grow a short-term relay interplanting there before the main crop reaches full size.

Nutrient Needs: The interplanted garden has a positive effect on soil nutrition and fertility. As we discussed in the explanation of relay plantings, crop diversification can reduce the nutrient demands made on garden soil. You should plan mixed relays so that vegetables removing one nutrient are followed by those requiring a different one. Use soil improvers such as beans and peas to replenish nitrogen absorbed by a preceding crop, thereby creating a short-term rotation. By the end of the season, the ground will need only a

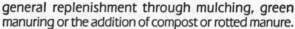

Nutrient needs are a prime consideration in determining interplanting combinations. If one crop is a heavy nitrogen feeder, interplant it with a nitrogen fixer

general replenishment through mulching, green manuring or the addition of compost or rotted manure.

Longer-term interplantings, in which crops remain together for most or all of the season, must also be carefully planned according to nutrient loss. This is especially important when you are growing high-nitrogen crops. Nitrogen is crucial for all plant growth and is the one element most likely to be in short supply in many soils. To raise two heavy nitrogen-feeders in one place for an entire season will not only result in poor crop returns; it might also have a detrimental effect on the soil.

Fortunately, many of the interplanting combinations that seem most favorable in terms of crop shapes and light needs are also good for the soil. The white clover strips used in a no-till garden are excellent interplantings for high-nitrogen feeding crops. Other soil-building legumes like beans, peas and soybeans make good interplantings, although they do not serve as pathways. Carrots, garlic, potatoes, turnips and similar root and tuber vegetables generally require little nitrogen, so they, too, do well with heavy feeders for all or part of the season.

Similarly, two crops removing mostly potassium (such as potatoes, leeks and carrots or turnips) should not be grown together unless the soil has been well enriched with wood ashes or similar fertilizer. Try to avoid interplanting phosphorus feeders as well, although some overlap won't matter since soils are generally well supplied with this nutrient and few crops remove tremendous amounts.

This kind of soil-wise interplanting, coupled with an overall rotation plan, lets the plants do most of your fertilizing work. Although midseason applications of manure, compost, wood ashes or other materials will still be important for some high-demand crops like corn, cabbage or tomatoes, your soil's general fertility will remain quite good with a minimum of work. As long as you begin the season with an organically rich, deeply spaded growing medium, the right plant combination will keep it fertile and loose. Once you've found an interplanting combination that performs well in your garden, keep those crops together in subsequent years. Rotate them as a unit from bed to bed every season, making sure that an entirely different combination follows them. If space allows, rejuvenate beds once every rotation cycle with a green manure crop of alfalfa, rye, soybeans or a similar soil-improving crop.

Companion Planting for Insect Control

Gardeners have long recognized that certain plants grown close to others are healthier than when they grow alone. This is partly due to simple diversification, but other, more complex factors are also involved. Simply stated, some plants seem to steer potential pests away from a main crop by serving as decoys to attract these insects. Other plants are insect repellents, discouraging pests from feeding in the area. A few may even be "nursery plants" that produce a combination of sugars and amino acids that attract insect predators and beneficial parasites, not pests. By planting these crops in close combination with others, it may be possible to prevent insect- and disease-related problems.

Research in the field of companion planting is just beginning at USDA labs, universities and private firms. At the Organic Gardening and Farming Research Center, studies have been carried out for several years with no clear results to report. So many factors are involved in cropping combinations and insect control that any definitive "proof" of a planting combination actually working may be hard to find. So far, the only convincing data has come from experiments with African marigolds. Roots of the marigold have been shown to secrete a powerful compound containing sulfur that repels root-knot nematode. Claims about marigolds' ability to repel the bean beetle, cabbage butterfly, whitefly and other insects, like claims for so many other companion planting combinations, have yet to be proven. The chart of vegetables, herbs and flower combinations in this chapter is, therefore, drawn from lore—not research.

Intensive Planting Arrangements

Once you have selected crops for interplanting, successions and relays, you must devise a spacing plan. Since each garden has its own unique topography, climate and soil, each will have slightly different requirements for a good layout. For best results be conservative, but not timid, in making your plan. A little creativity will lead to valuable discoveries and will also make your gardening lots more fun.

Planting arrangements can make or break the garden: too much space between crops destroys the effect of interplanting; too little space encourages disease, insect pests and competition for light, air, nutrients and water

Growing Beds: If you have constructed growing beds to raise some or all of your vegetables, you have many different planting arrangements from which to choose. In the rich, deeply spaded raised bed, plants can and should grow very close together. This creates a kind of "living mulch," a leafy canopy over the entire bed that shuts out weeds and retains moisture. But this closeness can be overdone, of course. Follow the spacing recommendations in the chart titled Between-Plant Spacing within Growing Beds, allowing even more space if your soil isn't quite as rich as it could be or if this is your first year working a bed.

The planting patterns described below will help you boost yields by fitting in the most possible plants per bed. Some are more efficient than others and a few are suited only to certain crops. Choose a variety of different patterns to create an interesting, productive series of vegetable beds. The diversity will also give you an opportunity to compare results of various arrangements

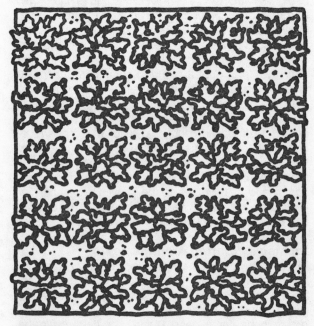

SQUARE-CENTER PLANT SPACING: *In this arrangement for rowed beds, plants in rows are spaced the same distance apart in all directions, forming a grid pattern.*

and determine the best setup for subsequent years.

Rowed Beds: The most common scheme for bed planting is a series of close rows. This scheme works equally well for single-cropped and succession beds, for relays and for permanent interplantings. As in any garden, position the rows so that the least shading occurs. Keep tall crops to the north and smaller ones to the south. Since pathways are unnecessary and soil is very rich, these bed rows are much closer together than those in a conventional garden.

To fill an entire bed with one crop, plant in rows spaced the same distance apart as recommended for plants within the row. The finished bed will have plants at equal distances, forming a grid pattern. This is known as square-center spacing.

You can plant some crops even closer together if rows are staggered, with each plant opposite a vacant space

EQUIDISTANT PLANT SPACING: *You can conserve space by staggering rows to have each plant opposite a vacant space in the adjacent row. All plant centers are the same distance apart.*

BETWEEN-PLANT SPACING WITHIN GROWING BEDS

Crop	Inches Apart	Crop	Inches Apart
Asparagus	12	Okra	12
*Beans, Bush	4	*Onions	4
*Beans, Pole	8	*Onions, Bunching	2
*Beets	2	*Parsley	4
*Broccoli	12	*Parsnips	4
Brussels Sprouts	15	Peanuts	12
Cabbage, Chinese	10	*Peas	2
Cabbage, Heading	15	*Peppers	12
*Carrots	2	Potatoes	10
Cauliflower	15	Potatoes, Sweet	10
*Celeriac	6	Pumpkins	24
*Celery	6	*Radishes	2
Collards	12	Rhubarb	24
Corn	12	Rutabagas	6
Cucumbers (vertical)	12	*Salsify	2
Eggplant	18	*Spinach	4
*Endive	15	Spinach, New Zealand	10
*Garlic	2	Squash, Summer	18
Kale	15	Squash, Winter	24
Kohlrabi	6	Sunflowers	18
*Leeks	2	*Swiss Chard	6
Lettuce, Heading	10	*Tomatoes	18
*Lettuce, Leaf	6	*Turnips	4
Melons (vertical)	15	Watermelons	12
Mustard	6		

*indicates crops that perform best in growing beds

in the adjacent row. This keeps all plant centers the same distance apart and takes advantage of the fact that plants tend to grow in circular, not square forms. It is known as equidistant spacing. Rows can be 1, 2 or 3 inches closer together when you use equidistant spacing. On a farm scale, using soybeans as a test crop, this arrangement has increased yields by as much as 25 percent. This is primarily because each crop is more exposed to the sunlight and because there is less overlap of rooting zones.

Minimum spacings are given in the Between-Plant Spacing within Growing Beds chart. However, in order to maintain these spacings, soil must be quite rich and moist. Compact crops such as greens, smaller members of the cabbage family, root crops, peppers and bush beans work best in such intensive arrangements. Use your own judgment and experience in intensifying the planting of other crops.

When growing more than one crop in a bed, row spacing becomes a bit more complex. To interplant, plant two or more crops within each row, or alternate rows of different crops. Spacing is generally easier to determine when rows are single-cropped, but both systems are useful and can be extremely space-efficient. When tall and short, deep-rooted and shallow-rooted plants are interplanted in alternating rows or within each row, spacing can be still closer and yields much higher than in a single-cropped bed.

To determine exactly how close to position rows and plants, average the space required by each plant. Thus, for a long-term, alternate-row intercropping of beans and carrots, add 4 inches (bean spacing) to 2 inches (carrot spacing) and divide by 2, thus establishing that the two rows should be 3 inches apart. If you're using an equidistant arrangement, the rows can be slightly closer. about 2 to 2½ inches, according to the Square-Center and Equidistant Spacing chart.

Interplanting within the rows is usually best for relay crops that will not be in the ground the entire time a main crop is growing. The practice, known as double-cropping, simply requires intermixing a fast-growing crop's seed with the main crop seed. For instance, you might mix radish seeds with beet seeds and sow them very thinly in rows spaced about 2 inches apart, as

Intercropping, combined with equidistant spacing and relays where possible, makes the best use of garden area

beets/radishes

39

SQUARE-CENTER AND EQUIDISTANT SPACING

Distance Between Plants	Distance Between Rows, Square-Center Spacing	Distance Between Rows, Equidistant Spacing
2 in.	2 in.	2 in.
3	3	2½
6	6	5
9	9	8
12	12	10
15	15	12
18	18	15
24	24	21

recommended for beets. The radishes will germinate before the beets, providing a marker for the row. You can harvest them about the same time you are thinning the beets for the second time.

Radishes, onions and leaf lettuce are all good within-row interplanting crops that perform well with most root crops, leeks and cole crops. Beans do well between potato plantings, onions between peppers, and early cabbage between tomatoes. In all of these combinations, plant the main, long-term crop in its suggested spacing, with the relay crop simply filling the unused areas during the early weeks or months of the season.

You can also maintain main crop spacings by using certain herbs as long-term intercroppings within a row. Although the herbs will usually remain in the ground all year, they require little space, thriving in the nooks and crannies between larger crops. Parsley, lemon balm, chives, thyme and rosemary are excellent interplantings between cabbage, lettuce or other crops. Mint performs favorably with tomatoes, and chamomile works well with onions. Consult the chart titled Herbs and Flowers for Companion Planting to find further suggestions for within-row interplantings of herbs. Often an entire row containing several herbs is a good addition to each growing bed. It not only requires little space but also could serve as a pest barrier, thereby protecting other crops.

INTERPLANTING WITHIN THE ROW: *The sizes and shapes of some plants, such as beets and lettuce, allow you to interplant them within the row. Plant the long-term crop according to suggested spacing and then fill in the spaces between them with the relay crop.*

Where you want long-term interplanting of two main crops within a row, it is necessary to average space requirements for the two vegetables and sow seeds accordingly. Make plans on graph paper, using 1-inch grids for easiest calculations. Use equidistant planting so that like crops aren't placed opposite one another. Do not crowd rows together; in a long-term interplanting, this could be disastrous. Instead, estimate row and plant spacings generously. Allow plants to touch one another but not to overlap or shade. In long-term interplantings particularly, soil fertility must be near optimum. Don't skimp on water. Side-dress with manure, or apply foliar sprays throughout the summer.

The more carefully you have selected planting pairs, the more successful the alternate-row and within-row intercroppings will be. Spacing can be closest when two crops are of complementary size and shape. When planting two of similar size, spacing can rarely be very close. Experience will teach you which plants benefit from very intensive culture and which prefer slightly

HERBS AND FLOWERS FOR COMPANION PLANTING

Herb	May Benefit	May Harm
Basil	Asparagus, tomatoes	
Borage	Squash, strawberries, tomatoes	
Catnip	Most crops	
Chamomile	Cole crops, onions	
Chives	Carrots, cole crops, cucumbers, lettuce	Beans, peas
Dill	Beets, cole crops	Carrots, tomatoes
Fennel		Most vegetables
Flax	Potatoes	
Garlic	Beets, cole crops, lettuce	Beans
Geranium	Corn	
Horseradish	Potatoes	
Hyssop	Cole crops	Radishes
Leek	Celery, lettuce, turnips	
Marigold	Beans, cole crops, cucumbers lettuce, potatoes, tomatoes	
Mint	Most crops	
Mustard	Cole crops	
Nasturtium	Beans, cole crops, cucumbers, potatoes, radishes, squash, tomatoes	
Onion	Most crops	Asparagus, beans, peas
Oregano	Squash	
Parsley	Asparagus, corn, tomatoes	
Petunia	Beans	
Rosemary	Beans, carrots, cole crops	
Sage	Beans, carrots, cole crops, peas	
Southernwood	Cole crops	
Summer Savory	Beans, onions, tomatoes	
Tansy	Cole crops, cucumbers, squash	
Thyme	Cole crops	
Wormwood	Most crops	
Yarrow	Most crops	

more room. Learn to judge a plant's mature shape and size so you can arrange seedlings as close as possible in your beds.

Blocks and Patches: Instead of running rows the length of the beds, you may wish to divide growing spaces into sections or blocks. These are easy to plant in rows going across or lengthwise along the bed or by broadcasting. They are simple to maintain and straightforward to plan. For a series of short-season successions, they are especially practical since the entire area is cleared before a new crop is sown. Salad crops grow well in dense, broadcast block plantings, as do any of the other low-growing compact plants or root crops. Using blocks for bed interplanting makes planting and harvesting simple, but take care to avoid monoculture. Block plantings can also serve as nursery areas where seeds are started and seedlings raised to transplant size before being moved to a permanent location. Some gardeners divide growing beds into equal-size blocks for convenient variety trials or other experiments.

Band and Border Plantings: Crops particularly suited to close spacing perform well when grown in 18-inch-wide bands within the beds, in wide borders around beds or in no-till strips. Root crops, salad greens and low-growing herbs and flowers are good candidates for band and border plantings. Where soil is a bit heavy, these growing areas can be tailored to specific plant requirements. For root crops, work in three parts top soil, one part sand, one part compost or peat moss and one part wood ashes. As you rotate root-crop bands

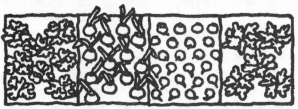

BLOCK PLANTING: *An alternative to planting in rows the length of the bed is to divide the growing bed into a series of small blocks or patches. This bed has each block planted in a different salad crop; two kinds of lettuce, radishes and onions.*

from bed to bed from year to year, the entire garden will eventually receive new, replenished soil.

Improving Yields in the Conventional Garden

Unless you have been gardening and fertilizing an area for many years, soil in the large, conventional, rectangular vegetable patch usually is not loose or rich enough to support intensive planting on a large scale. This doesn't mean, however, that your only option is to plant straight, single-file rows of individual crops. You can improve yields by using double rows and bands, circle-planting arrangements and other patterns. Successions, relays and interplanting can and should be carried out in the row garden almost as easily as in the raised bed. As always, different plans will be best for different crops in different growing areas. Below are some alternatives to

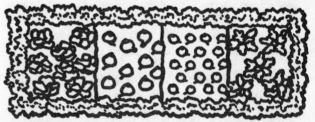

BORDER PLANTINGS: *You can plant a wide border around your growing bed with a low-growing crop that does well in close spacing. This bed, divided in blocks, has a wide border of parsley.*

the conventional rows and spacings that you can use in all or part of the garden. Many will not interfere with machine cultivation if your area is large and you wish to continue using a plow or tiller.

Double Rows and Bands:

You can significantly improve yields of compact crops that respond well to intensive culture, such as carrots, beets, onions, leeks, lettuce and spinach, by planting them in double rows or wide bands. This technique also works well in no-till strips. For double rows, place two rows close together with seeds or plants staggered as for equidistant spacing. Apply plenty of additional compost, rotted manure, wood ashes and other nutrient-laden materials, and space the two rows as close as the between-plant spacing recommended on seed packets. Separate these areas by ordinary garden paths covered with a thick mulch or boards to reduce compaction and moisture loss.

Even wider planting areas are possible if the soil is enriched and enough moisture is available. Broadcast seeds of the compact crops mentioned above within bands 6 to 36 inches wide, and thin them later to stand the suggested distances apart. An alternative is to plant crops in closely spaced rows within these band areas. Mulch well around the edges of bands to protect soil from the additional wear and tear it will get from thinning, weeding and picking. In addition to the compact crops, celery, celeriac, cabbage and bush beans also perform well in broad bands. Cut-and-come-again

If you are not yet ready to begin raised-bed intensive gardening on a large scale, successions, relays and interplanting are excellent options for making your existing vegetable patch more productive

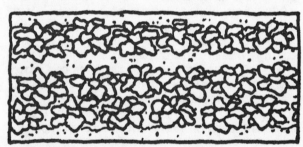

DOUBLE-ROW PLANTING: *Compact crops such as spinach can be planted to increase their yields by placing them close together in staggered rows as in equidistant spacing. As shown here, more spinach plants can be placed in a double row (bottom) than in a single-row planting (top).*

vegetables like chop suey greens, kale, turnip greens and Chinese mustard are also good choices since these plants give quick, abundant returns for the small amount of space they require. If you are able to supply abundant water and fertilizers, corn will also benefit from band planting, for the close spacing enhances pollination.

Interplanting can be accomplished within bands and double rows simply by alternating rows of different, complementary crops. Choose vegetables carefully for interplanting, and make the spacing quite generous. Don't follow spacings suggested for raised bed interplantings, which rely on quite different conditions than those found in the conventional garden.

Strip-Cropping: Strip-cropping is a variation on band and wide-row planting systems that is similar to no-till gardening. This technique is often used to improve conditions in large conventional gardens or in farm fields. In strip-cropping systems, cover crops grow in 3-foot-wide bands among other crops. You can use strip-cropping for erosion control, windbreak or soil improvement, depending on the crop you choose. Usually, soil-improving crops such as legumes, sod or hay are grown in these strips, but occasionally others are used. Experiments at the Organic Gardening and Farming Research Center over the past several years have focused on legume strips between rows of soybean or corn. In spring, legume cover crops such as yellow, red and white clovers, alfalfa and crown vetch are sown in wide strips, forming a dense sod that lives over the winter. The goal is to establish a cover that requires no weeding, controls erosion and offers soil enrichment while producing a bountiful hay or silage crop. Corn or soybeans are then planted in the strips, in double or single rows, and are allowed to grow to maturity. So far corn yields have been low, but soybeans have done quite well. It may be that once researchers hit upon the

STRIP-CROPPING: *A conventional rowed garden can be interplanted with strips of cover crops that can help to improve soil conditions and reduce erosion.*

right legume/crop combination, optimum yields will result in interplantings of corn as well as soybeans.

In a large home garden, the same combinations are worth investigating, particularly if you have a use for silage or hay. Plant crops within the legume sod strips, as in the experiments, or between them.

Other crops that perform well in between-crop strips are cut-and-come-again vegetables, such as the various Chinese greens and salad crops. They are useful in erosion control and as drainage paths on sloping, heavy soils. Grow corn or sunflowers as windbreaks, or use perennial plantings of bamboo or fruits for this purpose. You can grow simple rye grass or a similar sod crop in strips between band plantings or in double rows as replacement for ordinary pathways. Simply make the strips wide enough for your lawn mower, and you will be able to maintain clean, attractive walkways. This is certainly much simpler than weeding, and there will be a bountiful green manure crop to plow under in the spring should you wish to redesign your garden planting scheme.

All of these strip crops are easily incorporated into an ordinary garden plan. When worked into a crop-rotation system, they offer a good means of improving overall fertility with little work.

Blocks: Gardeners who enjoy the mathematics of gardening will find the square-foot technique of arranging plants efficient and easy to manage. With this system, described in Square Foot Gardening by Mel Bartholomew (Emmaus, Pa.: Rodale Press, 1981), the growing area is divided into 4 by 4-foot blocks with boards forming pathways between. Each of these equal areas is in turn divided into 16 1-foot-square blocks. The idea is to make gardening more organized, exact and, as in raised bed planting, to increase yields through intensive, precision planting. The gardener carefully positions crops within each square-foot block, each of which is temporarily marked off with string or a ruler. You place one cabbage in each square, for example, or nine bean plants, or 16 carrots. Spacings can be as close as those in raised beds since Bartholomew advises soil enrichment through the addition of topsoil, vermiculite, peat moss, compost and other materials.

Legumes, grass, hay and compact salad crops all make useful strip crops in the home garden

Carefully spacing and training crops to fit square-foot areas will produce a garden that is pretty as well as efficient

SQUARE-FOOT GARDEN: *Here the garden is divided in a very organized fashion that lends itself to intensive culture. Each growing area is divided into 4 by 4-foot blocks with pathways running between. The block is further divided into 16 1-foot-square sections for individual plantings.*

Interplanting may be carried out within each large block by simply growing different crops in alternating 1-foot squares. The standard block size makes planning for harvest very easy and enables you to build portable cloches that can be used wherever needed.

Circle Plantings: Circles are another attractive, effective way to grow vegetables. The circle was a typical planting pattern among the ancient Greeks and among North and South American Indians, for whom it symbolized completeness and harmony. Indians grew corn in the center of one circle, surrounded by larger circles of beans and either winter squash or pumpkins. Since each crop has different fertility needs, root zones and above-ground shapes, competition for light, water and nutrients is minimal. In fact, this particular combination actually improves the soil. Beans replenish nitrogen removed by corn; squash provides a ground cover that eliminates weeds and retains moisture. The circular shape improves corn's pollination so that all ears are filled with kernels. Furthermore, since spacing is fairly close, it's possible to plant several varieties of corn in a fairly small area. Cross-pollination will be unlikely.

Other crops requiring good pollination or partial isolation from surrounding plants also fare well in circle arrangements. This configuration encourages good air movement and reduces the border effect in plantings. Circles are a good mechanism for companion planting

CIRCLE GARDEN: *An attractive and effective way to grow vegetables is to plant them in 3- to 4-foot-wide circles. Planting corn in the center, beans around the middle band and squash on the outer edge is just one of the many planting variations.*

with insect repellent and trap crops. Surround circles of a main vegetable crop with "barriers" of marigold, onion, garlic or similar companions. Circles can also help to meet special crop nutrient needs. Peppers, cucumbers, melons and tomatoes, for example, can be more efficiently watered and fertilized if grown vertically in circle arrangements. Simply bury a clay pot or a number 10 metal can with holes pierced in the bottom and lower sides in the center of the planting circle. Partially fill it with compost or rotted manure and use it as a fertile "reservoir" during dry spells. When you add water to the container, it will percolate through the organic matter and carry nutrients directly to the roots of surrounding plants. Almost no moisture is lost to evaporation or to unplanted areas.

Make circles about 3 to 4 feet wide, or less for compact plants such as onions and carrots. Larger diameters will make weeding and thinning awkward. Follow standard spacing recommendations given on seed packets, placing crops slightly closer within the circle if you have enriched the soil and are providing it with a steady supply of moisture. For an ornamental circle garden, use an old wagon wheel as the planting circle, interplanting a variety of salad crops and low-growing flowers and herbs between the spokes. Old truck tires are sometimes used for circle container gardens that heat up early in spring for early crops of lettuce, greens and other spring salad crops.

Circle gardening has been fully described in Circle Gardening by Dr. Derald G. Langham (Old Greenwich, Conn.: Devin-Adair Co., 1978). Dr. Langham has done extensive tests on this method and advocates it as the most effective means of raising crops.

VERTICAL GARDENING TO SAVE SPACE

The vining crops that sprawl across the ground are the biggest space-wasters in the vegetable garden. Allowed to ramble to their hearts' content, crops like squash, cucumbers and melons produce little for the amount of space they require. You can improve their productivity per square foot by interplanting them with corn, but even this requires lots of room and does not eliminate problems of harvest and maintenance.

With a little care, however, most vine crops can be grown vertically. Training them upward on trellises and fences will produce maximum yields. Although individual trellised and staked plants will yield less per plant than those free to sprawl on the ground, more plants can be grown in the same amount of garden space, and total yields per space will be greater. For example, a squash plant needs 36 square feet to grow on the ground, but trained vertically it takes up only 4 square feet of ground. Single plants can be supported by stakes or wire cages, while entire rows can grow vertically along fences, trellises, arbors, pyramids or other structures.

Vertical gardening is no revelation to gardeners who grow peas and pole beans. Few would think of letting these crops trail over the garden floor, although they may produce quite nicely in that way. Even tomatoes, which are not natural climbers, are usually staked or trellised, even when space is not a problem. This not only provides more room for other crops but also makes weeding and harvesting much simpler with less chance of damaging the plant. Developing fruit stays cleaner, is less vulnerable to sunscald and is well out of the reach of slugs, snails and soilborne pests and diseases.

Vining plants trained to grow vertically produce more per square foot of garden space than plants allowed to sprawl on the ground

These same advantages will accrue by training squash, cucumbers, melons and pumpkins to grow vertically. Squash will remain unbruised and free of rot; cucumbers will actually grow straighter. Because you can do your harvesting without stepping on tender vines, you'll not only have more fruit in less space, but you'll have better fruit as well.

In the intensive garden, the vertical method is crucial to the productivity and health of beans, cucumbers, melons, peas, squash and tomatoes. Untrained, these crops are too sprawling for successful interplanting with other crops, particularly in a small raised bed. Letting them grow upward creates additional room for interplanting lettuce, onions and similar low-growing crops. Even in dry areas where close spacing is not advised, vertical gardening is an invaluable technique for making the most efficient use of available water and mulch and for preventing sunscald of fruit.

The problems associated with vertical gardening arise when poor techniques or unsuitable materials are used. Melons, pumpkins and squash in particular require very sturdy support that can bear up under many pounds of pressure. Select only sound materials for constructing trellises and fences. Do not use old, untreated wood, even if it seems a bargain; it's likely to come toppling down in mid-July along with your ripening fruit.

Many vining and climbing crops require no special care when grown on vertical supports. Others need to be constantly guided, pruned and perhaps even tied to the support since they are not natural climbers. Pole beans, cucumbers, melons and peas need no tying. As long as trellises, cages or similar structures are set up while the plants are still small, they will climb up of their own accord. Pumpkins, squash and tomatoes need more training, with tying necessary when string supports or mesh are used but not when they are grown in cages. Use bits of soft string or paper-covered wire twists to gently tie the runners or vines around the trellis. As you tie, lightly twist the vine around the trellis, but do not force it. This should be done every week or so, particularly while the plant is young.

Pruning is advisable in order to shape certain plants and train them to their supports. Some gardeners prune cucumber, melon and squash vines simply because the pruned plants seem to yield more succulent and sweeter fruit than those with more leaf and stem growth. Pruning these crops is similar to the "suckering" of

VERTICAL TOMATOES AND CUCUMBERS: *Climbing crops like these can be trained on a trellis. Tomatoes will need more training than natural climbers like cucumbers and melons. About once a week, gently twist the main stem around the trellis and fasten with bits of soft string. Both tomatoes and cucumbers need to be pruned regularly to keep lateral growth under control. Growing these crops vertically saves a great deal of ground space and creates an attractive "living screen."*

tomatoes: allow seedlings to develop their first leaves and flowers. As new runners begin to flower and set fruit, cut off their growing points and newest leaves. This will leave fruit on these runners but restrict leaf and stem growth to the main stem. By keeping these side runners well pruned, you will force the main stem to develop lush leaves. It will have a cluster of flowers and fruit at every node along its entire length.

Fruits of some cucurbits require special care when plants are caged or trellised. Melons, pumpkins and squash are so heavy that they may break the plants' stems and fall to the ground when ripe. For this reason, it is a good idea to select miniature dwarf melons and squash for vertical gardening. You will probably get higher yields per square foot from these plants, and you'll spend less time worrying about the weight of the

SUPPORTING FRUITS ON TRELLISES: *Cucurbits like squash and watermelon produce such large, heavy fruit that if not supported when trained to grow vertically, they will weigh down the vines and eventually break them. To provide support, place the fruit in a cheesecloth sling that is tied onto the top of the trellis.*

fruit. No matter what size you choose, you will need to provide added support for developing fruit with "slings" made from cheesecloth, garden netting or old panty hose. Use these to gently support fruits on the trellis or cage. Since they are made of porous, light material, the slings will permit aeration, and the fruit will develop normally.

A variety of supports useful for training beans, cucumbers, melons, peas, squash and tomatoes is described below. These tend to be far superior to the traditional wooden stake, and many are quite attractive additions to the garden.

Cages
Wire-mesh cages are a good alternative to staking, particularly for tomatoes. If you can find cages over 5 feet high, they also make good supports for cucumbers. Smaller, 3-foot-high cages are good for dwarf varieties of cucumbers and melons.

Look for ready-made cages in hardware and garden

stores, or constuct your own from heavy gauge 6-inch-mesh wire such as sheep fencing or concrete reinforcing wire. These materials are hard to cut and bend; don't buy them unless you have the proper tools. They are not cheap and will rust in a few years; in the long run, you may not save much over the cost of the manufactured cages.

One cage about 5 feet high and 18 inches in diameter will serve for a single tomato plant. Two cucumber plants, one opposite the other, about 1 foot apart, will grow in a single 18-inch-wide cage. Larger cages with diameters up to 3 feet can be used to support several plants set around the inside circumference.

Cages eliminate the need for most pruning and for tying, which can twist or bruise plant tissue; in addition, cages provide distributed support for the entire tomato plant

HOMEMADE TOMATO CAGES: *Wire-mesh cages are an excellent way to support tomatoes. The plants naturally lean on the wire, eliminating the need for tying. An additional stake placed next to each plant provides extra support.*

For tomatoes, set the cages in place when seedlings are planted out. Allow about 2½ to 3 feet between plants in the ordinary garden. In a double-dug fertile growing bed, space plants just 18 inches apart so that individual cages are almost touching. Along the outside of each one, drive a 6-foot pole into the ground and attach it for extra support. As the tomatoes grow, some branches may appear to need tying, but they really do not. The plants naturally lean on the wires with no training from the gardener.

For cucumbers, set up the cages as soon as the seeds are planted, and anchor the cages firmly to the ground with one to two stakes. Before planting, work in additional organic matter, or construct a 1-foot-deep trench 1 or 2 feet below the soil surface. Pack the trench with fresh horse or cow manure so that plants have the moisture and nutrients they require. Or bury a number 10 can in the center of a cage, partly filled with manure or compost, and use it as a watering trough, as described in the previous chapter in the section titled Circle Plantings.

Dwarf or miniature watermelons and cantaloupes will also grow in cages. Three-foot-high structures are usually sufficient for dwarf melons; they allow the gardener to reach over the top to harvest any fruit that grows bigger than the holes in the cages.

Bamboo Structures

Some of the lightest, yet sturdiest and easiest to manage supports for vertical gardening are made of lightweight bamboo poles lashed together to form A-frames and fencelike trellises. They are commonly used in oriental gardens and are inexpensive. Setting them up properly, however, takes some practice. Unless you set the poles firmly in the ground and balance them correctly against one another, the structures may come tumbling down when plants have their peak loads. Practice constructing a few bamboo supports before you try using them for the entire garden.

You can make a series of bamboo A-frames to support cucumbers in the rowed garden or intensive bed. Measure the length of the row, and multiply the number of feet by two. This will give you the minimum number of 6- to 8-foot-long poles you'll need to make the frame. Next, make the A's by using string to lash the tops of the poles together in pairs. Notching or drilling holes in the tops first will make the tying easier. Set the A-frames over the row every foot or so. The width of each frame's base

Bamboo trellises and supports are a common sight in city gardens in oriental neighborhoods. Bamboo poles are lightweight and easy to manage and are very sturdy as well

BAMBOO A-FRAME TRELLIS: *A series of light-weight but extremely sturdy bamboo A-frames can be used to support beans in a rowed garden or intensive bed. Beans are planted at proper intervals along the row and trained to climb the poles.*

depends on the crop you are growing and on the soil and moisture conditions; for beans, spread the frame 6 to 12 inches; for cucumbers, 12 to 24 inches. Wire or string connects the frames to one another along the sides. For additional strength, insert a straight pole at each end of the row. Plant one cucumber beside each pole, and train it to grow up the pole and out along the strings. Plant beans at the proper intervals along the outside of the row, and train them to climb up strings and poles.

You can also use bamboo to make a trellis for a row of peas. At planting time, set 3- to 4-foot poles in the ground every 6 inches along the center of the row. Run string to connect all the poles. Usually two rows of string are enough: one about a foot off the ground, and another a foot above that. However, more string will make it easier for the vines to climb without

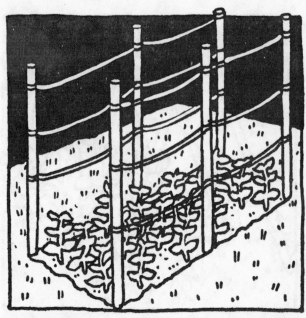

A CORRIDOR FOR PEAS: *Peas can be supported on horizontal strings run between bamboo poles. Two rows of string will do, but an additional row or two will make it easier for the vines to climb.*

your guidance.

Bamboo is not only a good support for growing crops; it also makes a fine ornamental and food crop to raise in your garden. Grown along one edge of the vegetable patch or bed area, it can form a windbreak or serve as an attractive backdrop to lower-growing crops. Young bamboo shoots are a delicious vegetable, older stalks may be cut off, stripped of leaves and branches and used for staking and other supports.

There are two types of bamboo, each with its own distinctive qualities. Monopodial bamboo produces large canes but is hard to control and tends to form a mat of underground roots and rhizomes. Sympodial bamboo is the preferred type, for although its canes are smaller than those of monopodial bamboo, it has no underground runners and can be easily grown in clumps or rows.

Trellises
You can either make your own wood or metal trellises

or buy them at a local garden shop. Generally, the manufactured trellises are designed for roses or other flowers and are really too light for vegetables other than beans or peas. You will have the most success if you construct your own frames for the heavier crops.

Trellises can be entirely wood, entirely metal or a combination of an outer wood or metal framework with netting, wire or string attached for the crops to climb. Those made entirely of wood or metal tend to be cumbersome and difficult to store unless they are collapsible or can be knocked down at the end of the season. To make your trellis collapsible, either lash the pieces together or join the sections with wire, hooks, hinges, pegs or bolts.

Large trellises of wood or metal can be hinged or bolted together to make them collapsible and easier to store over the winter

How to Build a Tepee Trellis: Tepee and pyramid trellises made of saplings or lumber are fairly sturdy and are appropriate for beans. Some will also support

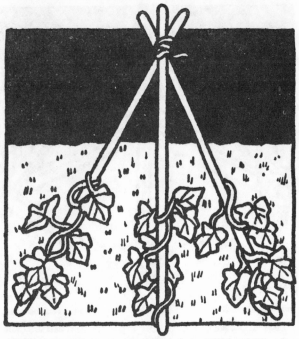

TEPEE TRELLIS: *A simple tepee trellis will adequately support pole beans. By adding horizontal rows of wire around the tepee, you can also use it to grow cucumbers, squash and melons.*

cucumbers, melons or squash, although not always in the most space-efficient manner. To construct a simple tepee that will support many bean plants, lash three or four 8-foot poles together at the tops. Again, if you drill holes or cut notches in the tops, you will have a sturdier structure. Use a hatchet to sharpen the bottoms of heavy poles, spread the structure and set it firmly in the ground. Width of the base should be about 2 to 3 feet, with several pole bean seeds planted around each pole. If you add crossbars or wrap heavy wire around the tepee, you can use it to grow cucumbers, melons and squash as well.

Pyramid trellises give crops good exposure to the sun and make efficient use of space

How to Build a Pyramid Trellis: You can use pyramid trellises for pole beans, cucumbers, melons or squash. However, be forewarned that they take longer to construct, and once built they're cumbersome and

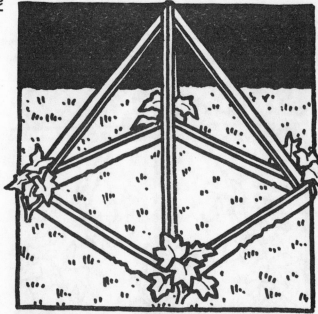

PYRAMID TRELLIS: *Although pyramid trellises can be cumbersome to work with, they are extremely sturdy and do an excellent job of supporting all vertically grown crops. The seeds or transplants are planted inside or outside the trellis, next to the base boards.*

difficult to move unless they can be knocked down at the end of the season.

To build a sturdy pyramid trellis, select oak, redwood or construction lumber treated with copper naphthenate. Make a base by nailing together four 1 by 2 boards, two of which are 92 inches long and two of which are 94 inches long. At each corner, nail a 5 by 5-inch square of plywood. These corner platforms will support the pyramid skeleton. Next, select four 89-inch-long 1 by 2 boards as the main frame supports. Each board must be cut to the proper angle so it will fit the base and, with the others, form a point at the top. A protractor will help: cut each piece to an angle of 48 degrees at one end and 42 degrees at the other. Bolt the 42-degree ends to the corners of the base, and connect the 48-degree ends to a 1 by 1 by 3-inch block of wood at the apex. To complete the pyramid, wrap wire or twine around the frame, and plant seeds on the inside, just beside the base boards or on the outer edge. Follow the proper spacing recommendations for the crop being grown.

How to Build a Two-Dimensional Trellis: By far the simplest to make and easiest to manage trellises are two-dimensional wood or metal frames with netting or wire for the plants to climb. They are easy to assemble and to knock down for winter storage. Two-dimensional trellises are able to support virtually every crop, from peas to heavier melons or squash, with little adjustment in design. As the most space-saving type of trellis, they may be incorporated into a conventional rowed garden, intensive growing beds or any other vegetable garden scheme.

The framework for these trellises should be sturdy, but not so heavy that it cannot be easily moved. Standard electrical conduits, ½ inch in diameter, can be threaded and used with plumbing elbows to make an upright frame that will withstand years of weathering and frost heavage. Water pipe and metal fence posts make equally strong and durable frames that you can leave outside all year.

Frames constructed and used at the Organic Gardening and Farming Research Center are made of wood. Although not as long lasting as the heavy pipe or metal ones, they are more portable, an important factor in the

Use two-dimensional trellises either singly, in groups of four as an arbor, arranged in a zigzag pattern or as a straight fence

61

vegetable garden, where rotation, relay planting and successions make frequent changes necessary. If you bring them in for the winter, the wooden frames will last for many years. Use redwood or cedar 2 by 4's or standard construction lumber thoroughly treated with copper naphthenate.

Researchers find that, no matter what material is used for the framework, the most convenient size is 5 feet high and 4 feet wide, with an additional 2 feet allowed for pounding into the ground. These dimensions make it easy to lift and move the trellis without handling the delicate mesh. Joints should be lapped and bolted or held together with wood screws. A top crossbar, although not absolutely necessary for lightweight crops,

TWO-DIMENSIONAL TRELLIS: *Good for any type of garden, conventional or intensive, these trellises save space and are easy to build and move. Each trellis is made of a frame of 2 x 4s, 5 feet high and 4 feet wide with a top crossbar. Twine, chicken wire or nylon netting is hung on the frame to support the crops. You can put up several of these trellises side by side and train plants to form a living screen to hide a garage or shed.*

helps the netting and wire hold their shapes and makes for a sturdier trellis.

Choices for material to be used to support the crops range from inexpensive twine to chicken wire or nylon netting. Twine or wire will perform well for crops that are pruned to a single vine. Chicken wire will serve for peas or beans, but its holes are much too small for the larger vegetables, which might blossom and set fruit within the mesh. Because you can't reach through it to the other side, one-sided picking is impossible, making it less desirable in many gardening situations. While sheep fencing and concrete reinforcing wires have larger openings, they are too stiff for easy attachment to the trellis frame.

By far the best option in terms of economy, handling and durability is nylon garden mesh. Unlike the metals, which often rust after a few seasons, nylon garden mesh will remain attractive and strong. It is quite easy to stretch onto the frame, and, if you use the right size, it can support many different vegetable crops.

Netting is available through seed suppliers and garden stores in sizes ranging from 1½ by 1½-inch mesh to 6½ by 6½-inch mesh. The smaller sizes work best for peas and beans, which can climb up it with little training. On the larger 4- to 6-inch mesh, they must be trained and intertwined around the nylon every few days in order for them to climb. However, the small holes of the 1½-inch mesh make it impossible to reach through for picking; instead, you must pick from two sides. Larger mesh is often stronger and is recommended for vegetables with large vines and fruits, including cucumbers, melons, squash and tomatoes. Some crops will require intertwining around the nylon mesh, but this is not a problem because there are generally only a few runners to handle.

Use staples to attach the mesh to the wood or metal frame. Although it is not necessary to start the mesh at ground level, you will get better results if you do. Small pea, tomato or pole bean plants can be easily knocked over in a storm before they have taken hold of the trellis material, resulting in broken stems and otherwise damaged plants. For this reason, it is recommended that mesh start within 6 inches of the soil surface and continue to the top of the trellis frame. Pull it taut as you staple it so that the stretch is removed.

Another option for supporting plants is to hang string or wire from the top bar of the trellis frame, on which pea and bean vines can climb. For best results, either bury the bottoms of the strings in the soil or peg them; this will cause them to stay put while the plants are still young. To make the trellis stronger and to provide more room for vines, attach a bottom crossbar, and zigzag the strings between it and the top bar.

STRING TRELLIS: *Another form of the two-dimensional trellis is to zigzag string from the top bar to the bottom crossbar of the trellis frame. Pea and bean vines are then left to climb the strings.*

IDEAS FOR ORGANIC FERTILIZING

Incorporating compost and manure into the soil is a standard, basic technique for organic gardeners. With practice and experience, everyone tends to work out the methods and materials that suit them best. In this chapter are some tips on methods and materials that could help make your soil enrichment program more rewarding or more convenient.

Alfalfa

Alfalfa is one of the most effective, practical soil amendments gardeners can use. It can be grown as a nitrogen-fixing cover crop in bed gardens and conventional garden patches. It also makes a fine green manure crop, and it can even be used for strip-cropping between plantings of vegetables. Grown in place of part of your lawn, a lush, green patch of alfalfa will not only reduce the amount of grass you have to cut but also will provide a source of fresh green material to chop and use as a rich garden mulch.

Work at the Organic Gardening and Farming Research Center has shown that adding fresh, green, chopped alfalfa to the soil in fairly small amounts produces high yields in many crops. The most effective rate of application is about 1½ ounces (or 1 cup) of fresh alfalfa per 100 square feet of garden area. When spread and worked into the upper layers of soil, it improves soil structure and adds nitrogen.

As an organic mulch, you can't beat fresh, chopped alfalfa. It is especially effective when weather is hot and soil nitrogen levels are fairly low. Applied 6 inches deep, it settles to form a dense, 3-inch layer that admits

In addition to a regular soil-improvement program built around compost and manure, the use of nutrient-rich mulches or cover crops, custom-blended organic fertilizers and convenient liquid plant foods can provide an extra boost for heavy-feeding crops

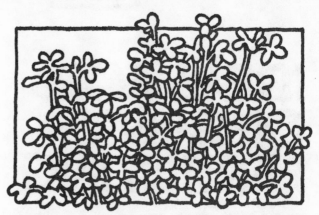

MULTIPURPOSE CROP: *Grown as a nitrogen-fixing crop, a green manure crop, used for strip-cropping between vegetables or in place of a lawn, alfalfa is one of the best soil-builders you can grow.*

rainwater, controls weeds and keeps the ground cool, moist and loose. Since it is possible to apply too much green, chopped alfalfa to already rich soils, mix it with other materials when mulching root crops or others with low nitrogen needs.

To grow alfalfa, you must have a well-drained, sunny location with a soil pH of about 7. Add potassium and phosphorus the first year and every three years thereafter. Nitrogen supplementation is unnecessary and may even spur weed growth. Mow the planting whenever it starts to bloom, collect the cuttings and use them for mulching or composting. If you make the cuttings close to the ground, weeds will not become a serious problem, and the stand will develop winter-hardy roots.

Recipes for Balanced Organic Fertilizers
Soil that is well stocked with organic matter and minerals can often support healthy vegetables without additional help from fertilizers. However, it is advisable to give plants a little boost when cropping is continuous. This is especially true in gardens where available nutrients may be scarce. By feeding plants nitrogen, phosphorus, potassium and other elements in organic forms they can readily absorb, you not only keep them healthy but also maintain high soil reserves. This cuts down on the amount of spring and fall fertilization you will need to do later.

Since individual organic and mineral substances usually supply only one or two major nutrients, you must mix several together to create a well-balanced fertilizer. This can be tricky if your goal is to make an all-around organic fertilizer with a specific N-P-K (nitrogen-phosphorus-potassium) analysis. It requires some information on release rate and percentage composition of organic ingredients as well as a few calculations. Most of us prefer to skip this bit of paper work and use the "little-of-this, little-of-that" approach, which is only successful as long as our luck holds out.

Gardener Mel Bartholomew has come up with an especially good mix with a reliable analysis of 2.6–4.9–2.4 that works for all vegetable crops. He suggests using his formula full-strength in the spring as you prepare the soil and half-strength (mixed with an equal portion of compost or sand) as a monthly supplement. The recipe is as easy as one, two, three: 1 part blood meal, 2 parts bone meal, 3 parts wood ashes and 4 parts composted leaf mold. For leafy vegetables requiring lots of nitrogen, increase the blood meal to three parts, giving an analysis of 4.6–4.3–2.0.

Two other well-balanced fertilizers that organic gardeners can rely on are: 1 part wood ashes, 1 part animal tankage, 1 part soybean meal and 1 part bone meal (with an analysis of 4–7.2–2.2) and a mix of 2 parts blood meal, 1 part rock phosphate and 4 parts wood ashes (with an analysis of 4.3–6.8–4.8).

Among organic liquid fertilizers, the most cost-effective ones are the compost and manure teas made from finished compost and/or fresh barnyard manure steeped in water. To make a bucketful of this wonderful stuff, place several trowelfuls of manure or compost in a burlap bag, along with a few tablespoons of rock phosphate, wood ashes, seaweed, chopped alfalfa, blood meal, bone meal or any other substance you wish to add. Tie the bag securely, and immerse it in a bucketful of water. Cover the bucket to keep out breeding mosquitoes. Stir the brew every day or two so that water flows through the bag and dissolves the nutrients. After one or two weeks, the tea will be a rich, dark brown color, ready to ladle onto seedlings, maturing crops and germinating seeds. Use it full strength (it won't burn plants), or dilute the mixture until it is the color of weak tea.

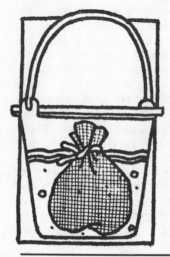

MANURE TEA: *To make this useful brew, suspend a burlap bag filled with manure and other organic amendments in a bucketful of water and let it steep for a week or two. The result is an economical liquid fertilizer that can be fed to germinating seeds, seedlings and maturing crops.*

Horticulturist Lawrence D. Hills, director of the Henry Doubleday Research Association in England, recommends a similar tea made from chopped, fresh comfrey. To make this potassium-rich fertilizer, place about 14 pounds of chopped comfrey in a 20-gallon container, then fill it with water. The mixture will ferment and, within about four weeks, you can drain a clear liquid from the bottom and use it to feed beans, cucumbers, tomatoes and other crops that require lots of potassium and small amounts of nitrogen. Analysis of the finished comfrey tea is approximately 3–1–7.

Liquid fertilizers like manure tea, seaweed solutions and fish emulsions are especially effective when applied to plant leaves rather than being poured on the soil surface

Foliar Sprays

Although some nutrients must definitely be present in the soil around plant roots, it is also beneficial to spray some in liquid form directly onto plant leaves, where they are quickly absorbed. Studies show that foliar feeding is a quick way to correct obvious nutrient and mineral deficiencies. Leaves are more selective than roots and will absorb only the minerals needed, preventing any imbalance from developing. Foliar sprays work well in conjunction with slow-release soil fertilizers, providing a boost to crops of all types and at all stages of development. In the intensive, interplanted garden where crops are closely spaced, foliar spraying is often the only means of providing fertilizers without damaging growing plants.

Use weak solutions of manure tea, comfrey tea, seaweed or fish emulsion for foliar applications. Seaweed solutions are probably the best sources of minerals and minor elements, supplying aluminum, boron, calcium, cobalt, iron, magnesium, manganese, molybdenum, sodium, sulfur and a host of other nutrients. Comfrey tea is best for potassium deficiencies. Fish emulsion, although smelly, will correct phosphorus and nitrogen deficiencies. Spray plants every three to four weeks, being sure to use a solution about 50 percent as strong as that recommended for soil applications.

Feeding from Reservoirs

If you garden a large area and feed crops every few weeks during the summer, consider constructing a holding tank for liquid fertilizers. A tank eliminates the need to mix a fresh batch every time crops begin to flag and then wait while it steeps. It insures a ready supply when plants need it, and it frees you to complete other tasks in that busy season. Your reservoirs can be small, for feeding one or two plants on a nearly automatic basis, or they can be large enough to hold food for the entire garden.

Plants can be fed and watered automatically with mild fertilizer solutions from a reservoir

How to Make a Small Reservoir: To make a small reservoir for one or two plants, use a widemouthed plastic jug, a hose fitting, grommet and washer and nut. Cut a hole close to the bottom of the jug, insert the grommet and hose fitting and attach with a washer and nut on the inside. Next, jam the end of a short piece of hose over this hole, and plug the other end with a rubber cork or a similar type of stopper. One inch from the end, cut several tiny holes, each about the diameter of a finishing nail. Fill the jug with filtered compost tea, fish emulsion or other liquid fertilizer that has been diluted to about one-half to one-third its normal strength. Replace the lid, and punch holes in the top to allow air to enter. Place this container in the garden beside the plants you wish to fertilize. The nutrient-rich water will slowly drip out of the hose, providing both water and fertilizer at once. Although there is some danger in overfeeding your crops when using this sort of automatic system, you won't have any problems if you keep the solution quite weak and move the container to other plants every week or two.

FEEDING FROM A SMALL CISTERN: *For frequent feedings of liquid fertilizers, a small cistern can be made for one or two plants. A gallon milk jug with a hose attached at the bottom is filled with the desired liquid fertilizer and placed beside the plants to be fed. The fertilizer is left to trickle out the small holes that have been punched in the hose, feeding and watering the plants at the same time.*

How to Make a Large Reservoir: To hold a season's worth of liquid plant food, build a larger reservoir. Although, with the help of gravity, this container can be used as a large-scale version of the small automatic system described above, it is more useful as a simple holding tank from which you can draw plant food as needed.

Use any container that will hold water and has not previously held toxic substances. An old-fashioned rain barrel is ideal if you are lucky enough to have one. Large industrial plastic or steel drums are easier to find; if sturdy, they make excellent reservoirs.

To convert a steel drum, begin by cutting out the top, using either a saber saw fitted with a metal-cutting blade or an oxyacetylene torch. Discard the top, and wash the drum thoroughly. If you wish, paint the inside with rustproofer or boat paint, although this is not absolutely necessary.

Turn the barrel on its side and stabilize it in some way. Using a ball peen hammer, flatten a section of the

The longest lasting and most accessible containers for reservoirs are standard 55-gallon steel drums

drum's side, about 2 or 3 inches from the bottom. Wear ear protectors, because this is a very noisy job. Taking your time, make a smooth, flat area about 4 inches in diameter where a steel nipple and faucet will be inserted.

Sandpaper the flat section to remove all rust and paint. Take a steel nipple, ¾ inch in diameter, about 6 inches long and threaded on both ends, and stand it upright against the drum, just 2 inches from the bottom. Use a pencil to trace around the nipple, and drill a small hole in this circle to admit a metal-cutting saber saw blade. Cut just inside the lines you have traced so that the nipple may be screwed snugly into the hole. Once you have cut the right-sized hole, thread on a ¾-inch conduit nut and a rubber washer. Crawl into the drum and screw the nipple into the hole, creating the tightest fit possible. Seal the outside of the hole, around the nipple, with silicone sealer, and screw on a flange-type faucet with a ¾-inch female threaded opening. Finally, in order to prevent clogging, use a stainless steel hose clamp to cover the inside of the pipe with a small square of fiberglass screening. Set the drum on a platform high enough to fit a watering can or bucket under the faucet, and paint the outside with rust-resistant paint.

DRUM RESERVOIR: *A large steel drum can be used to hold a season's worth of liquid fertilizer. Fitted with a spigot, the fertilizer is prepared in the drum and can be easily removed when needed.*

Grow-It

NEW DEVELOPMENTS IN PEST CONTROL

By juggling your planting times so that crops are harvested before the heaviest insect feeding period, or are at least large enough to sustain damage, you can minimize pest problems

Organic gardeners pride themselves on the natural health of their gardens, and rightly so. With the right crop varieties, planting schemes, soil preparation, fertilizing and watering, pests and diseases are not likely to be much of a problem. Healthy plants take care of themselves, and hungry insects are kept at bay. Pests that do enter the garden to feed on crops are eaten by birds, toads and insect predators or handpicked by the watchful gardener.

Still, there are times when even the best gardener meets his match and wishes for some more sophisticated ways to eliminate harmful insects without destroying the good ones. A few holes in the cabbage leaves are tolerable, but when whole rows of onions are destroyed by maggots or when borers ruin an entire crop of summer squash, patience wears thin. That is the time when the techniques of chemical gardening—of pesticides, herbicides and other prepacked cure-alls— begin to look pretty tempting, if only for a moment. Organic methods, as most of us know them, seem too haphazard, too downright unscientific.

The fact is, however, that natural pest control is founded on scientific principles and is fast moving into the forefront of horticulture and argriculture. As scientists have come to recognize the dangers of many chemical pesticides and their ultimate failure in controlling insect damage, they have been forced to look more closely at some of the naturally occurring pest repellents and other agents. The result is a whole new array of techniques

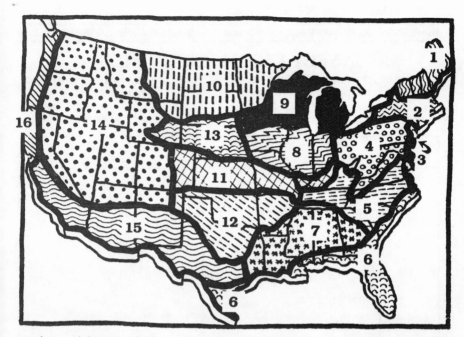

and materials, as well as some additional information on the more well-known organic controls that gardeners have been trying for years.

Below we will discuss some of these new, safe insect and disease control measures. A few are preventive measures, while others are natural pesticides that are safe and inexpensive to use. Add these techniques and materials to your present methods, and you'll have the ultimate pest defense system for your vegetable garden.

INSECT EMERGENCE TIMES: *Each of the 16 zones represent areas where emergence times of various potential pests are similar. Use this map along with the table on pages 74–80 to plan the planting dates to avoid harmful pests.*

Time Your Plantings to Miss the Bugs

Most gardeners already know that it's good to stagger planting dates in order to extend the harvest. But did you realize that this can also help some crops avoid hungry pests? Most insects do their major damage to crops during a fairly short period in their life cycle. They appear at about the same time every year as long as there is no drastic change in the weather, and they often begin feeding immediately. After this initial feeding period, they may metamorphose, lay eggs and die, with a new generation emerging soon afterward.

The Insect Emergence Times chart is based on information gathered from entomologists throughout the U.S. It lists the emergence times of several pests you'll want to avoid in the garden, but it is by no means complete. By keeping records of the dates you first notice these and other insects in your garden, you can create a more precise, expanded time chart.

INSECT EMERGENCE TIMES

To use this chart, first look at the map to find your region. Say, for instance, a reader in Tennessee has problems with striped cucumber beetles every year. She finds that she's in Region 5, and that, according to entomologists in her area, the beetle emerges in early May. Rather than set out her tender young cukes at the same time, she may

Region	Bean Aphid	Pea Aphid
1	No problem	End of May
2	No problem	April
3	No problem	April
4	June 1	April
5	May and June	May
6	Year-round. Worst from October to May.	On peas in fall, winter and spring. Worst November to February.
7	Mid- to late March. Active year-round.	Mid- to late March
8	When warm weather arrives	Active May 1. Most abundant during June.
9	June	April. Most destructive in May.
10	Rarely a problem	Builds up in May and June, again in fall
11	No problem	Active in April
12	No problem	March and April
13	No problem	May
14	Active June through August	Active mid-May through June; mid-September through October
15	Spring and fall	Does not apply
16	Active mid-May through July	May and June

decide to wait until mid-June, after the beetles have emerged, found her garden lacking in cucurbits and moved on.

The information for each region comes from entomologists whom we contacted in that region.

Asparagus Beetle	Colorado Potato Beetle	Striped Flea Beetle
Mid-June	First week of June	June 1
May	Late May	Mid-May to early June
Late April to early May	Early May	Late April to early May
Early May	Early May	Early May
Late April to early May	May	April. Active through summer.
Does not apply	March. Active through May.	Spring, summer and fall
Does not apply	Does not apply	March and April
May	April and May	Late May
Early May	Mid-May to late June	May and June
May and June	June	Does not apply
Late April through May	Late April through May	April and May
Early spring	Does not apply	When seedlings come up. Active all season.
Mid-June	Mid- to late June	June
Active early May through June	Mid-June	Active all summer
Does not apply	Does not apply	Does not apply
April through June	Late May to early June	Does not apply

[continued on next page]

INSECT EMERGENCE TIMES

Region	Japanese Beetle	Corn Earworm
1	Mid-July	Late July
2	Late June. Active through October.	August
3	End of June	June; peaks in August
4	End of June	July and August. A problem after September 1.
5	June	Mid-June
6	Does not apply	North: Summer, early fall. South: Early spring, late fall.
7	Does not apply	1st generation: June. 2nd: mid-July (most destructive).
8	Most abundant in July	Spring and early summer
9	Does not apply	End of July. Active through August.
10	Does not apply	Mid-July through August
11	Does not apply	Migrates late June. Causes damage through September.
12	Does not apply	Plant so corn silks between June 25 and July 1
13	Does not apply	Causes most damage in July
14	Does not apply	Early July
15	Does not apply	Does not apply
16	Does not apply	June and July

Gypsy Moth	Tomato Hornworm	Mexican Bean Beetle
Eggs laid May 10	Does not apply	Early to mid-June
1st generation: May	Late July to early August	Mid-June
Eggs hatch late April to early May	Does not apply	May
Eggs hatch May 1	June	June 1
Does not apply	Late June	May
Does not apply	April to September	Does not apply
Does not apply	Mid-June	Does not apply
Late April through May. Full-grown larvae by late June.	May or June. Eggs hatch a week later.	Late March in south, June in north
Does not apply	Late June to early July	Does not apply
Does not apply	Does not apply	Does not apply
Does not apply	July and August	Does not apply
Does not apply	June	Does not apply
Does not apply	Late June	Does not apply
Does not apply	July and August	Adults in May. Larvae feed May to July.
Does not apply	Does not apply	Does not apply
Does not apply	Late May through June	Does not apply

[continued on next page]

INSECT EMERGENCE TIMES

Region	Northern Corn Rootworm	Spotted Cucumber Beetle
1	Does not apply	Mid-June
2	Does not apply	Mid-June
3	Does not apply	May and June
4	Eggs hatch mid-June	June
5	Does not apply	Early May
6	Does not apply	A continuous pest
7	Does not apply	Does not apply
8	Larvae in spring. Adults in July.	First 70°F day
9	Larvae in late June. Adults in late July.	Mid-May. Active through season.
10	Eggs hatch June. Adults emerge late July.	June
11	Does not apply	Early May
12	Does not apply	Does not apply
13	Larvae in June	May
14	Does not apply	Does not apply
15	Does not apply	Does not apply
16	Does not apply	Does not apply

Striped Cucumber Beetle	Squash Bug	Squash Vine Borer
Mid-June	Does not apply	Does not apply
Mid-June	June	Mid-June. Most active in July.
Mid-May	Late May through June	Adults: May. Larvae: second week of June.
End of May	June	Mid-June
Early May	About May 1	Late June
Does not apply	March. Active through August.	August through October
Does not apply	June	Late June to July 1 on garden crops
May	June	Adults lay eggs when vines run
Does not apply	Does not apply	Does not apply
Does not apply	Does not apply	Late June to early July
Does not apply	When squash is fruiting. Active through fall.	Early to mid-July
Does not apply	Late May	Late May through June
Does not apply	Late spring	July
Does not apply	August and September	Does not apply
Does not apply	Does not apply	Does not apply
Does not apply	April and May	Does not apply

[continued on next page]

INSECT EMERGENCE TIMES

Region	Cabbage Looper
1	Mid-July
2	Late June to early July
3	July. Active through September.
4	1st generation: June
5	Late April
6	North: Early spring to late fall. South: Active year-round.
7	Early March
8	Moths lay eggs in spring
9	Early August
10	After mid-June
11	When cabbage comes up
12	Active year-round. Most destructive in fall.
13	May
14	June. Active until frost.
15	September and October
16	April and May

Pelletize Seeds

You can protect vegetable seeds from being eaten by birds, mice and insects by giving them a special coating before you plant them. Treat corn seeds with a thin mixture of tar and gasoline to repel birds and mice. Mix other seeds with clay and push them through medium chicken wire, then allow them to dry before planting. To make very small seeds easier to sow and to protect them from wireworms and other soil pests, dampen them and mix them with agricultural gypsum before planting.

Pelletizing is also useful in inoculating legume seeds with nitrogen-fixing bacteria. Binding the inoculant to the seed with a sticky, protective material will improve the bacteria's performance. Soak legume seeds in water overnight in order to enhance germination and to give bacteria more moisture at planting time. Combine the inoculant with a mixture of water and molasses to form a runny paste. Molasses should constitute about half of the total amount of liquid suggested on the inoculant package. Stir the seeds into this mixture, making sure that each is evenly coated. Next, scoop out the treated seeds, and dump them into a dry bucket containing some sifted rock phosphate powder. Shake the bucket back and forth so the seeds are thoroughly coated, then remove the finished seeds and spread them on a tarpaulin to dry in the shade for several hours. When the pellets are dry and hard, plant them. The rock phosphate will form a protective coating, and the sweet molasses will provide food for the nitrogen-fixing inoculant bacteria.

Introduce Insect Predators

Virtually every garden magazine contains ads selling lady beetles, praying mantids and other "good bugs" guaranteed to rid your garden of certain pests. They are bought by the thousands and released into vegetable patches to gobble up all those pesky, unwanted critters. But do lady beetles, praying mantids and the rest really do their job? Who's to say that they won't move on before you have gotten your money's worth? In short, are the mail-order beneficials really worth the cold hard cash?

Most of them are, provided you can keep them where they are most needed. Problems occur when your garden can't sustain a huge population of imports, or when the insects arrive with migration already on their minds. To keep them, you need the right garden setting and plenty of the insects' favorite foods. Crops should be diversified, some weeds should be present, and lots of pollen- and nectar-producing ornamentals should be

To keep insect predators in your garden, be sure there is enough food for them to eat

nearby. Sometimes, even when these are provided, beneficial bugs still decide to fly off to neighboring fields and gardens. Nothing short of a greenhouse seems to keep some beneficials where you want them.

Yet, with the right precautions, you may have success with certain mail-order insects. The following discussion lists the more common predators and parasites as well as their effectiveness and proper use in the garden.

Lady Beetles: Lady beetles are sold by liquid measure, with about 80,000 adults to the gallon. A pint or two might seem to do the job of ridding your garden of aphids, whiteflies, scale and various insect eggs, but it isn't that easy. Commercial ladybugs are notorious wanderers, bent on migrating as soon as they are released in their new home. In the greenhouse, they succeed as controls, since they can't escape. In the home garden, success is less common.

There is one way to encourage lady beetles to stick around, though. Dr. Kenneth Hagen, an entomologist at the University of California at Berkeley, suggests that preconditioning and special feeding for several days help prevent the lady beetles from migrating right away. Since suppliers don't do this themselves (none of the ones with whom we've talked precondition their shipments), gardeners must do it themselves. It may sound crazy to be pampering your lady beetles in this way, but if you're serious about importing beneficials, it is worth the effort. It beats having 20,000 or more flit off to your neighbor's field, leaving your garden infested with aphids.

For each quart of ladybugs, you'll need a tight screen cage that's about 4 feet wide, 6 feet long and 4 feet high. You will also need a special high-protein food called wheast, which is a by-product of the cheese industry. Wheast can be purchased as Formula 57 from CRS Company, P.O. Box 7585, St. Paul, MN 55119. Since it is only available in 100-pound quantities, a good idea is to organize a group of gardeners willing to purchase the wheast collectively and then divide it into smaller quantities among yourselves.

When your package of ladybugs arrives in the mail, place it in the refrigerator's crisper box, where the insects will stay moist and cool. Take the screen structure you have built and place it in the garden, over any vegetation. Next, empty the ladybugs into the cage. In a few hours, feed them a mixture of 1 pound of wheast and 1 pound of sugar dissolved in a gallon of water. Spray this food through a clean pump-type hand sprayer onto the foilage. Continue feeding the beetles every day for five days. At the end of that time, they will have established themselves in your garden, and the cage may be removed. The beetles will be ready to feed on aphids and lay eggs on foliage.

Praying Mantids: These insects are overrated in their predatory abilities. Sold in egg cases containing 100 to 300 mantids, they develop into awkward, ironclad creatures with powerful legs to hold their prey and sharp jaws to eat them. Unfortunately, their fierce appearance suggests that they're much more aggressive, hungry predators than they actually are. Although it is true that mantids are natural enemies to scores of garden pests, they are not really able to control infestations. The problem lies with their appetite and disposition. Praying mantids don't much care what they are eating; these passive creatures are just as happy to munch on a few lady beetles as on pesky squash bugs. They simply sit on leaves and wait for something to happen by. Each may eat only a few bugs per day, with no guarantee that even these will be pests.

Ladybugs can be an effective means of controlling garden pests, but praying mantids are overrated as a biological control

Green Lacewings: These insects are the best mail-order predators you can buy. Also called aphid lions, the slender green larvae feed on aphids, mites, thrips, leafhoppers and caterpillars, while the winged adults eat only pollen and nectar. As long as your insect pest population is large enough to sustain them, they will feed in your garden a long time before moving elsewhere.

Most companies sell lacewings in the egg stage. When they arrive, place them in a dark, 70°F room until the eggs have hatched and you can see the tiny larvae crawling along the bottom of the carton. Then tear open the container and allow the larvae to crawl onto garden foilage. Spread them out, for they will begin to feed on one another before they notice the aphids and other tasty morsels your garden provides. Since the larvae have no wings, you can rely on them to stay right in your garden, often eating about 400 aphids each before reaching adulthood.

Parasitic Wasps and Flies: Another mail-order option is the purchase of parasitic beneficials. Unlike predators, parasitic wasps and flies kill by laying eggs on host insects. Their hatching larvae feed on the pest, gradually weakening and killing it. Anyone who has ever seen a cabbageworm or tomato hornworm with papery white capsules on its back has seen parastic beneficials at work; the capsules will eventually hatch into tiny Trichogramma wasp maggots that destroy the worm.

In addition to the Trichogramma wasps, there are numerous other parasites, each of which feeds on just one or two insect pest types. Encarsia formosa is widely used in the greenhouse to control whiteflies, and Chelonus curvimaculatus for control of potato tuberworms. Pediobius foveolatus lays eggs on Mexican bean beetle larvae and is now being tested by researchers at the Beneficial Insect Introduction Laboratory in Beltsville, Maryland.

Unfortunately, while these and other parasitic insects have been found effective in greenhouses and on large farms, they are not always successful in controlling pest problems in the home garden. Most gardens are too small to supply the parasites with all the prey they need. Problems also arise when the gardener does not know exact genus and species of the problem insect; since parasites usually lay on just one species, it is essential that the pest be properly identified. Finally, there are sometimes problems in releasing the parasites at the correct time so that pests are in the right stage for receiving eggs and parasites are ready to lay.

In short, unless you have a large garden of an acre or more and have clearly identified a population of a specific pest, don't rely on these insects for control.

Make Sprays from Backyard Ingredients

We're only now beginning to discover that the safest and often most effective pesticides can be found right in our own gardens. Two new pest control methods, which are being tested at Rodale's Organic Gardening and Farming Research Center and elsewhere around the world, can be made at home with some common plants or insects, some water and a blender.

One technique guaranteed to keep your neighbors guessing is the bug-juice spray made by pulverizing the very insects that are eating plants and spraying the strained mixture back onto the foilage. The idea is to repel hungry survivors and force them to look elsewhere for their food. Although it sounds downright wacky, it's a method supported by many gardeners who swear by its success. One Florida pest control specialist used bug juice to rid a 100-acre peanut patch of pests; an Arizona woman used it to solve a serious problem with skeletonizers on her grapes; a Kentucky gardener ground up Colorado potato beetles and used the strained liquid to protect potatoes for the rest of the season. All in all, gardeners claim that bug juice works with over 20 different insects, including cabbage loopers and other caterpillars, aphids, slugs and wireworms.

On the scientific front, bug juice remains pretty unconvincing. Several researchers have reported negative results when bug juice is used, and one controlled study in South Africa showed that cutworm extract actually attracts rather than repels cutworms. At the Organic Gardening and Farming Research Center, experimenters have tried the technique on Colorado potato beetles, aphids and other insects, but the results were at best inconclusive. Scientists offer several explanations for the apparent problems. Bug juice can become contaminated with salmonella bacteria if it is not used within a few hours after being made, or is not frozen for storage. Allowed to remain on plant leaves, it might also promote bacterial or fungal growth, possibly harming the plant even though it repels the pests.

If, in spite of the lack of scientific support for this method, you would like to try it, you'll need to collect about one half cup of the target pests. For very small insects like aphids or white flies, a quarter cup or even a spoonful is enough. Place the bugs in a blender with two cups of water and "puree" until you have a homogenized mixture. Strain, and use the clearish liquid immediately, freezing any remaining portions. Since the juice can be diluted up to 250 times without losing its supposed strength, add a bit more water so you will have some spray left for reapplication after a rain.

A similar technique involving "plant juice" has a somewhat wider acceptance among scientists and seems to show more potential for future research. The source of this spray is any nonpoisonous plant which does not seem to be attacked by the problem pest,

Remember that just because a plant has a strong smell does not mean that it will repel insects — some aromatic plants may even attract them

or which is known to repel it. The plant leaves, stem, or flowers are ground in the blender with a bit of water, and the resulting liquid strained for use as a repellent spray on infested plants. Scientists at Cornell University suggest that the method may work because certain plant compounds do actually repel specific insects. If the same compounds can be suspended in water and sprayed onto other crops, the insects will go elsewhere to feed. Plant juice extract from an exotic Indian tree is being successfully used against the Japanese beetle, and extracts of certain pines are used against apple moth and codling moth in New Zealand. Gardeners from Alaska to Florida have also found the method to work against mites, various caterpillars, and other insects.

Rodale experimenters have spent two years testing various sprays and dusts of plant origins. Commercial materials such as rotenone, diatomaceous earth, and Tri Excel were tested, as were homemade sprays of catnip, coriander, eucalyptus, mayapple, tansy and pyrethrum (made from Chrysanthemum cinerariaefolium flower heads). They were used against Colorado potato beetles, green peach aphids and cabbageworms. Sprays of catnip, coriander, nasturtium, rotenone, mayapple and diatomaceous earth all caused a significant reduction in the beetle populations on potatoes, particularly early in the season. This result suggests that the solutions tend to prevent migrating adults from laying eggs on the sprayed plants. Sprays used against the aphid and cabbageworm seemed to have no effect. Experiments in subsequent summers will continue to examine these and other sprays that might be used to repel major garden pests.

To make a plant-juice spray of the sort used in the Rodale experiments, select a nonpoisonous plant which is not infested with the insect. For best results, choose only smooth-leaved plants; hairy or prickly ones tend to repel insects by their physical barriers, not by their taste or smell. You need an aromatic crop, one with an oil which can be sprayed on infested crops. To every part of packed leaves or flowers, add two to five parts water, and whisk the mixture in the blender until thoroughly combined and chopped. Strain the liquid, adding a small amount of Ivory liquid or similar mild soap to keep the ingredients in suspension.

To apply plant and bug juices, use a simple hand-held

sprayer that produces a fine mist. If you have a large garden, and lots of crops to spray, you may wish to invest in a harness that will hold the tank on your back.

Interplant with Insect-Repellent Plants

Folk wisdom has long recommended companion planting with various aromatic herbs and other plants as a way to prevent insect infestations. Researchers have concluded that African marigolds are indeed repellent companions, keeping nematodes under control, but there is no scientific evidence showing that the scores of other well-known companion plants are actually effective. Tests by Rodale seem to suggest that interplantings must be very close in order for the beneficial companions to have any effect on pest populations. Even then results can't be guaranteed. There are numerous variables involved in such experiments, so it will be some time before conclusive evidence is available.

Results so far have been conflicting, but there are indications that interplantings of coriander, nasturtium, onions, oregano and tansy do have an effect on certain insect pests. Cucumbers interplanted with oregano showed fewer striped cucumber beetles during at least part of one season. Potatoes interplanted with tansy and then planted with eucalyptus had fewer potato beetles. However, certain planting combinations actually seemed to attract insects, indicating that plant-insect interactions are very complex and need further study before we can fully understand them.

Grow-It

EXTENDING THE GROWING SEASON

F or most gardeners north of Florida and east of San Diego, growing vegetables is strictly spring-time-summertime business, with fall reserved for cleanup and winter for catalog browsing. The growing season officially begins with the last spring frost and ends with the first fall one, although a few daring gardeners might extend it one or two weeks in either direction. We eat freshly picked vegetables only a couple of months each year; the rest of the time, we buy vegetables doused in preservatives and shipped in from several hundred miles away.

Recent advances in horticultural technology make it possible for gardeners throughout North America to grow vegetables earlier in spring and later in fall

True? Yes, but it need not be. With just a few dollars, you can devise or buy well-designed cloches and plastic mulches that tack six weeks onto each end of the growing season. By growing some of the newly discovered and developed cold-hardy crops (see the next chapter, Adding Variety to the Vegetable Garden), you can further extend your growing season. Finally, for a gardening season that continues right through the winter, you can build a solar growing frame.

Each of these options is affordable and practical. Each will pay back its initial investment cost the first time you bite into a fresh, homegrown winter salad.

Solar Growing Frames
These structures are revolutionizing home gardening by making it possible to raise and harvest crops outside in the dead of winter. Unlike the standard cold frames which they resemble, solar growing frames actually work: they are able to maintain adequate growing conditions all winter long, even in the northernmost

88

regions of the United States and most of Canada. Unlike greenhouses, they require no special heating systems, cost nothing to operate and are relatively inexpensive to build. Solar growing frames are much smaller than conventional greenhouses and are also more efficient. Air and soil temperatures remain above freezing with very little fluctuation on a daily basis.

There are many different designs for solar growing frames, most resembling slightly oversized, insulated cold frames. Noted solar architect Leandre Poisson created one of the first solar growing frames, a triple-glazed, fully insulated structure that supports vegetable crops during even the harshest New England winters. Set in the ground with its top angled southward to capture maximum sunlight, Poisson's frame has an 8 by 5-foot growing bed, which can provide enough fresh vegetables to feed four adults all winter long. Three recycled 30-gallon oil drums, painted black and filled with used motor oil or water, provide thermal mass.

POISSON GROWING FRAME: *Solar growing frames make the dream of fresh vegetables in winter a reality. This growing frame, invented by Leandre Poisson, can provide four adults with fresh vegetables throughout the winter. Thirty-gallon oil drums filled with water or used motor oil collect heat during the day and release it slowly at night to maintain suitable growing temperatures.*

They absorb solar heat during the day and radiate it back into the growing beds at night.

Working with the same principles, Rodale researchers have come up with their own solar growing frame that requires no heat collectors. In extensive tests over the course of several winters, they evaluated the designs of 16 different growing frames, each slightly different in size, shape, materials, location or some other important feature. Then, combining the most workable features

RODALE'S SOLAR GROWING FRAME: *Rodale researchers have developed their own growing frame that requires no heat collector. The rectangular plywood frame, measuring 4 feet wide by 8 feet long, sits on a masonry foundation, providing approximately 27 square feet of growing area with a 2-foot-deep soil bed. The lid to the frame has a fiberglass-polyethylene double glazing. The frame is insulated with Styrofoam and has a urethane foam shutter covered with aluminum foil to add further insulation at night. It is an inexpensive structure that can be built at home with common tools.*

with the most efficient yet economical materials, they created an inexpensive growing frame that can be built at home with common tools. Specific building plans, along with horticultural suggestions, are provided in the Rodale Plans book Solar Growing Frame, edited by Ray Wolf (Emmaus, Pa.: Rodale Press, 1980).

Light, rich and well-drained soil is essential for healthy

crop production in a growing frame. While it should be light enough to assure good drainage, it must also be able to hold moisture. Since crops are planted intensively in very shallow soil, fertility must be optimal. Soil sterilization or pasteurization is not necessary, particularly if seeds are not being sown directly in the frame.

For the best growing frame soil, combine a rich topsoil having a pH of 6 to 7 with compost or leaf mold, rotted manure and sand or peat in the following amounts: one part topsoil, two parts compost or well-rotted leaf-mold, one part well-rotted horse manure and sand or peat as needed to lighten the soil. Mix up enough soil to fill the growing bed to a depth of 12 inches. On the south side of the structure, the lowest end, the soil should be 2 to 3 inches below the bottom of the glazing. This allows for optimum light levels.

The best plants for a solar growing frame are high in vitamins and rich in flavor, produce abundantly over a long period of time and thrive in cool temperatures

Almost any cool-season crops will grow in solar growing frames. Broccoli, cabbage, endive, lettuce and spinach are obvious choices, but other less conventional vegetables, described in the next chapter, Adding Variety to the Vegetable Garden, are much more productive.

You'll get the best results by sowing seeds indoors under lights or on a sunny windowsill for later transplanting to the growing frame. With this method, you can provide the soil warmth necessary for rapid germination and can monitor the young plants' progress during the most crucial stages. Harvests will be two to three weeks earlier than with directly sown crops, making it possible to raise more vegetables during the season. Start seeds five to seven weeks before you wish to transplant them to the solar structure. In transplanting, choose only the healthiest, stockiest seedlings, and space them closely in staggered, interplanted rows. Place short crops in the front of the frame and taller ones at the back. To avoid leaf burn, which occurs when plants touch the cold glazing, refer to the seed company's "estimated heights at maturity" when you plan the planting arrangement.

Fertilization is necessary since most of the cool-weather crops are heavy nitrogen-feeders and are growing in a rather stressful environment. But don't overdo it. Accumulation of salts is a danger here as much as it is in container or greenhouse gardening; strong fish emulsions and other high-salt fertilizers should be used sparingly. Frequent feedings of weak manure or

Portable glass or plastic cloches can be placed over plants to collect the sun's warmth during the day and radiate it back to plants at night, thus extending the growing season during the cooler weather of spring and fall

compost tea are better than fewer applications of more potent fertilizers. Apply the solution at transplant time, then again every two weeks throughout the season.

Supply water sparingly as well. While new transplants may need daily watering, depending on temperatures in the frame, older plants usually require water only once a week. When air temperatures inside the frame drop below 34°F for several weeks, plant growth slows down, and much less moisture is required. During these periods, water only every two weeks. Always water early in the morning on a sunny day so that the leaves will be dry by evening.

Throughout the winter there are many days when outside temperatures rise well above freezing and direct sunlight causes temperatures in the frame to reach 85° to 90°F. This much heat encourages disease and places stress on most cool-weather crops, particularly newly transplanted ones. Whenever temperatures reach this level, venting is essential. Open the frame door 4 to 6 inches, or even more if the outside air temperature is above 50°F. Close the doors again if cloud cover develops.

With a well-built growing frame, it is unlikely that even a first-year winter gardener will encounter serious problems. With good soil, the right plants and care in providing air, nutrients and water, harvests should be plentiful and delicious.

Cloches

Much used in England but virtually unknown here until recently, these simple plant protectors are required equipment for efficient gardening. Though they offer minimal protection from spring and fall frosts, they are very efficient at capturing heat during the day and reradiating it to plants at night. This greenhouse effect encourages rapid growth and development, thereby stimulating early production of summer vegetables and hurrying the ripening process of some fall crops. Cloches also enable northern gardeners to grow some warm-season vegetables—such as cucumbers, melons and tomatoes—that might not otherwise mature in the short season. By the same token, gardeners living in milder areas where winter temperatures seldom drop below freezing can use cloches to raise hardy and half-hardy vegetables year-round.

There are two types of cloches: those that cover

individual plants and those that cover entire rows or beds. Individual plant covers or "hot caps" are usually conical in shape, often with small ventilation holes in the peaked top. They are easy to set up and remove but are not usually used for long-term crop production. Larger cloches are more efficient in warming soil and keeping it moist for germinating seeds. A-frames, tunnels and other structures that cover rows and beds of plants promote consistent growth over a large area and can be used to carry entire crops through from seeding to maturity.

Almost every gardener has improvised a cloche of some sort at one time or another. A cone made of newspaper or a plastic jug with the bottom removed might be set over a tender pepper plant when frost threatens, or a sheet of plastic could be used to protect some ripening tomatoes in late fall. These aids may offer some protection to tender plants, but often such last-minute makeshifts cause more harm than good. Plants may be injured when ventilation is inadequate or when materials are poorly chosen. In short, many of the cloches we toss over our garden plants are neither

PLANT PROTECTORS: *Plant protectors come in all shapes and sizes. They serve to capture heat during the day and release it at night, thus increasing temperatures around the plants, which hastens their growth and development. From left to right, a fiberglass pyramid cone, a plastic jug and a heavy wax paper cone are just a few of the many types of cloches.*

> *A good cloche or hot cap must admit light, retain heat while allowing air to circulate, provide easy access to the plants inside and be of a durable material*

effective nor durable. Much more sophisticated ones are needed both to keep plants alive as temperatures drop and to promote their growth.

Some excellent manufactured row covers and hot caps are sold through garden stores and general mail-order catalogues, but it is not necessary to buy one in order to have a good one. A few companies sell plans for constructing your own cloches. With some basic knowledge of what it takes to make a successful cloche, you can design structures that are made to measure for your garden's beds, rows and individual plants.

Rodale's garden researchers have tested many of the manufactured cloches along with some homemade structures. They have found that good light transmission, high heat retention, proper venting, stability, durability and easy access for watering and plant care are the most important features of workable hot caps and row covers.

Cloches can be made from just about any translucent or transparent material, from wax paper to glass. They should let in as much light as possible, especially if they are used during winter to raise plants rather than simply to protect them for a few days or weeks. Opaque papers and plastics are fine for temporary covers, but don't try to use them over a long period of time. For the best light transmission, choose glass. It is long lasting and attractive, and it will not fade over the years. However, since it is expensive and breakable, many gardeners find it impractical for their needs. Good alternatives to glass are the new plastics, acrylics and fiberglass materials that have been specifically designed for use in solar structures. Although these become scratched and lose some of their transparency over time, they are lightweight, cheap and easy to handle. Select only those plastics that won't break down from ultraviolet radiation and that can withstand some of the ravages of air pollutants.

None of these materials retains heat particularly well, but then cloches, as a rule, cannot offer very effective protection against subfreezing temperatures. With a two-layered plastic cloche, however, you may be able to raise night temperatures as much as 5°F, which might be enough to keep some plants from being damaged. Double layering does, however, greatly reduce light levels under cloches. Before you choose your materials, carefully consider just how you intend to use the cloches. Will they be temporary frost guards or long-term growth chambers?

Oddly enough, the real problem with many cloches isn't low temperatures; it's high ones. Because overheating can quickly kill plants, effective and quick ventilation is a must. Hot caps covering individual crops are easy to remove on warm days or to open from the top. Long tunnel cloches must have a more formal means of venting hot air. It should be possible to open the ends or sides without having to dismantle the entire cloche. Check manufactured covers for adequate heat escapes. In your own designs, use hinges in appropriate places, leave flaps open in places or make doorways.

It is not at all unusual for temperatures under a hot cap or row cover to reach 85° or 90°F on a bright, sunny winter day

Since spring and fall are often windy seasons, cloches and hot caps must be securely anchored to the soil. Many manufactured units have no supporting stakes and will blow away unless the gardener devises something. Even glass cloches, heavy as they are, need some type of anchoring, particularly if they have sharp angles which could catch the wind. Where possible, use soil, wire pins, stakes or heavy weights to stabilize all these devices. These anchors will extend their life and cause less damage in your garden.

Keeping row covers and hot caps well anchored should not, however, make it impossible for you to water, weed, plant or harvest. A frustrating problem is having limited access to plants once the covering has been set up. In some cases, the entire structure must be raised in order to care for plants. Usually, if adequate ventilation is supplied, the same openings can be used for access.

A few of the cloches that were tested at the Organic Gardening and Farming Research Center stand out as being especially practical and worthwhile. Of the hot caps, the most successful were those made of wax paper and anchored to the soil with a stake. Equally successful was the fiberglass "Solar Cone"™, designed by Leandre Poisson and sold through Solar Survival (Box 275, Harrisville, NH 03450). The wax paper caps are cheap and may last two or more seasons. Early in the season, they offer good frost protection and, because they keep the soil moist, need not be removed for watering. Later, as temperatures rise, the top may be snipped off for ventilation and watering purposes. The Poisson cone has the advantages of being extremely long lasting and quite heavy so that it anchors itself in place. Made of sturdy fiberglass sheets, it is pyramidal in shape (just in case pyramid power really does make a difference).

Tests showed that glass panes held together in an A-frame position with special hinges called Rumsey clips make the best tunnel cloches. Since their ends are open, ventilation is no problem and yet, surprisingly,

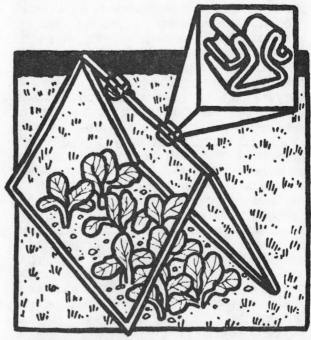

A-FRAME CLOCHE: *Glass panes held together with Rumsey clips in an A-frame position make an excellent tunnel cloche.*

plants are still well protected from wind and insects. The light-transmitting quality of clean glass surely has a lot to do with the success of such frames.

Among the homemade row covers, 6- to 8-mil polyethylene stretched over metal, wood or plastic frames is very effective. As long as the frame is strong enough to resist rain and wind and the plastic is snugly attached to the frame, such easy-to-make cloches prove versatile and effective. Plastic cloches can be made in

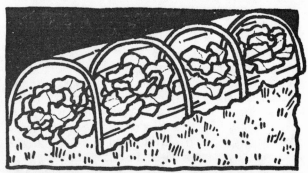

TUNNEL CLOCHE: *A sheet of polyethylene can be stretched over wire hoops to cover an entire row or bed.*

tunnel shapes by stretching the plastic over metal hoops laid over the rows or beds in Conestoga-wagon fashion, or in A-frame shapes with a kind of pup-tent design. By planning ahead, you can make permanent frames that stay in place year-round. After the plastic is lifted in summer, the frame comes in handy as trellising. It can also be used with netting or cheesecloth to shade young plants.

Plastic Mulches
A great deal of research that has been done on mulching with polyethylene film indicates that it is very useful for raising soil temperatures by at least a few degrees. Although they do not provide the soil-building or even long-term water-holding advantages of some organic materials, don't overlook plastics as important materials for extending the growing season. Many of the newer types are biodegradable; they will break down in a month or two, after which the plastic mulch can be replaced with organic materials. Other plastics are so durable that you can save and reuse them for many seasons.

Clear polyethylene film, 1½ mils thick, will have the greatest effect on soil temperatures, raising them some 10° to 20°F in spring before plant leaves are big enough to cast any shade. Polyethylene film is recommended as a mulch for early sowings of peas, radishes, lettuce, beans, corn and potatoes, particularly in areas where the growing season is very short. However, weeds grow rampantly under the clear film, so it may be wise to apply an additional mulch of dark plastic or organic matter on top of the clear plastic once summer has started.

Black plastic will warm spring soil about 5° to 10°F and does not promote weed growth. Again, a 1½-mil thickness is suggested for easy handling and durability.

Lay plastics on the garden after the soil has begun to dry in spring. Place one sheet on an area to be covered, and weight it down with stones. Dig a 3-inch trench around the perimeter. Place the edges of the plastic in the trench and cover with the soil you have removed. Punch a few slits or holes in the plastic so water can infiltrate. At planting time, cut slits for seeds or transplants.

PLASTIC MULCH: *Black plastic used as mulch can warm the soil temperature in spring 5° to 10°F while reducing weed growth. The plastic covers the growing area and has slits cut in the material to allow water to penetrate and for planting seeds and transplants.*

Windbreaks

In many vegetable gardens, wind causes more damage than subfreezing temperatures. It erodes and dries the soil, causes mechanical injury to tender crops and significantly lowers the effective air temperature. Even light winds take their toll on the vegetable patch by seriously retarding plant development and reducing yields. Although an occasional gentle breeze is helpful in clearing the air of harmful fungi and bacteria, gardens and growing frames should be sheltered from persistent winds with a windbreak.

The best windbreaks are openly woven structures that filter the air rather than stop it. A windbreak that is solid as a wall will simply redirect the wind and possibly increase its destructive powers. Far better protection is provided by a hedge, a row of trees or fencing material. Plantings offer a permanent solution to wind problems, while fences are inexpensive, temporary protectors.

Choose fencing that is about 80 percent solid for best protection from heavy winds. Height will depend on the angle of the prevailing winds and the need to maintain adequate light levels within the garden. Of

Consider a windbreak if your growing area is located near a large body of water, in a wide open field or along a ridge or gap

FENCES AS WINDBREAKS: *Wind can cause irreparable damage in the garden as it erodes and dries the soil, lowers the temperatures and causes tender plants to break and tumble over. A fence near the garden can help reduce the force of the wind and protect the growing plants.*

course, where space is limited and the fence must be quite close to the garden, it should be no higher than 5 feet, or it will probably cut off a large amount of light. Choose a snow or picket fence for an area with these limitations. Where the fence can be placed 10 or more feet from the edge of the growing area, it can be higher and will provide a more effective windbreak. As a general rule, a good windbreak fence will protect an area that is ten times as deep as the fence is high, depending on the angle of the wind. Thus, a 10-foot lath fence may cut a 30-mile-per-hour wind to about 15 miles per hour for a distance of up to 100 feet.

The same rule applies to natural windbreaks of shrubs and trees. Plantings of various conifers, such as arborvitae, cedar, fir, hemlock, pine, spruce or yew, make excellent windbreaks, as do Siberian elm, Russian olive, honey locust, red willow, amur privet, poplar and viburnum.

NATURAL WINDBREAKS: *Trees can act as a natural wind barrier to protect the garden. They should be planted 50 feet from the garden in a position where they will block the most persistent prevailing winds.*

Bamboo makes an excellent summer windscreen that will also provide some delicious spring eating. Consult your county agent for a list of windscreen plants that do well in your location.

Plant windbreak trees about 50 feet from the garden area so they do not compete with garden plants for light and moisture. Shrubs may be somewhat closer, up to 5 feet from the garden, depending on their height, density and rooting depth. In planting trees and shrubs, consider not only their height but also their mature width. Space them far enough apart so they can develop healthy branches and will form dense growth. Protect young trees and shrubs with snow fencing or other temporary wind protection until they have become well established.

Position natural or fence-type windbreaks where they will be most effective, then monitor over an entire season to establish the direction of the most persistent or prevailing winds. Usually these winds will come from the west or north, although local conditions may prove otherwise.

ADDING VARIETY TO THE VEGETABLE GARDEN

Most vegetable gardens are woefully predictable—a couple of rows of beans, a block of corn, some cucumbers, cabbage, broccoli, squash, melons, pumpkins, onions and, of course, the ubiquitous tomatoes. Aside from the occasional eggplant, celery or soybean, every gardener's seed order must resemble every other gardener's, year after year after year. Seed companies, it seems, must resort to Madison Avenue hoopla in order to coax us into adopting new foods. Ten or 12 years ago, full-color center spreads of zucchini squash convinced us to grow that "unusual" vegetable. More recently, edible-pod peas and spaghetti squash have been promoted on catalog covers with the result that they have now become staples in many of our gardens.

Gardeners are by nature curious people, so it is surprising that we are so conservative when it comes to choosing crops. We will go to all kinds of trouble to devise new ways to protect early tomatoes or cleverly do in striped cucumber beetles. We'll try new fertilizers and experiment with different planting techniques. If only this imagination were used in choosing the very crops we raise, vegetable gardens would become the most fascinating—not to mention productive—places in the world. Our vegetable vocabularies would increase

Try some different vegetables in your garden to add exciting new flavors to meals

tenfold, and we would be sharing planting tips on cardoon and recipes for scorzonera souffle.

If you wish to raise any out-of-the-ordinary crops that the major seed companies don't happen to be promoting, you'll have to do some searching. Begin by reading all of your seed catalogs, past and present, from cover to cover, noting the fine print and back pages, for that is where you'll most likely discover the more unusual vegetables. Once you have exhausted those sources, request catalogs from some of the seedhouses listed in Seed Sources for Unusual and Cold-Tolerant Crops, found at the end of this chapter. Start with companies located in growing areas similar to your own, but don't be afraid to order seeds from faraway sources. Often only one or two companies sell a particular seed in this country; as long as the crop can be grown in your climate and soil, the home of the seed is of little importance.

An evening's search through a few specialty catalogs will leave you wide-eyed at the number of crops you've never heard of, much less considered growing. There are oyster-flavored root crops, edible chrysanthemums, weird claw-shaped pod vegetables and winged beans. There are plants from generations past and from halfway around the world. Many are gourmet vegetables you can't afford to purchase in the supermarket and never imagined could be grown in your own backyard.

In this chapter is a discussion of just a few of the more interesting vegetables that do well in a wide range of North American climates. For more information on most of these crops and on many other out-of-the-ordinary vegetables, consult Anne Halpin's Gourmet Gardening (Emmaus, Pa.: Rodale Press, 1981) and Nancy Bubel's Vegetables Money Can't Buy but You Can Grow (Boston: David Godine Publishing Co., 1977).

Unusual Perennial Vegetables
At least two vegetables deserve a place in the perennial patch, right beside the asparagus and rhubarb. These are sea kale, which slightly resembles asparagus in taste and use, and comfrey, a highly nutritious plant with hundreds of culinary, medicinal and garden uses.

Both sea kale and comfrey will thrive in most parts of the United States and Canada, particularly if protected with a thick winter mulch

SEA KALE AND COMFREY: *Two unusual perennial vegetables well worth trying. Sea kale (left) resembles asparagus in taste and use and comfrey is highly nutritious with many uses.*

Although sea kale grows fastest from root cuttings, you can also grow it from seed. In early spring, sow seeds 1 inch deep in rich fine soil either outdoors or in flats. Thin established seedlings to stand 6 inches apart, and maintain the stand throughout the summer and fall. Mulch well in late autumn. Very early the following spring, rake away the protective mulch to allow the young shoots to emerge. At this time you can move the plants to a permanent location, set 3 feet apart in well-drained, neutral, nitrogen-rich soil. Keep the bed weeded and well watered, and mulch each fall to assure winter survival.

After two years, when plants have developed sufficient strength, begin harvesting some spring shoots. In late March or early April, shoots will begin to pop up. As their tips emerge, cover them with inverted flowerpots (with the holes blocked), or simply mound dirt over them. These coverings will blanch the plant tissue. After several weeks, harvest the tender 5- to 7-inch-long shoots. After harvesting, clean the bed and apply nitrogen-rich manure and other organic fertilizers.

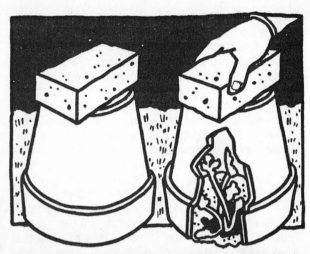

BLANCHING SEA KALE: *Cover the emerging tips in early spring with an inverted flower pot that has a brick on top to cover the drainage hole. The tender 5- to 7-inch shoots can be harvested several weeks later.*

Continue to weed and water the plants throughout the summer. If you are attentive, you'll be able to maintain a single bed of sea kale for about five years.

Comfrey is probably the most care-free of all vegetable plants. Also known as boneknit, some people grow it for its medicinal value, while most know it only as chicken feed. What many don't know is that comfrey is also an excellent leafy vegetable, similar in taste to spinach yet yielding continuously. It is a fairly large, bushy flowering plant if allowed to grow unattended, but you should keep it well trimmed if raising it as a vegetable crop. Comfrey readily establishes itself. It may even begin to take over your garden, so select an area where it will have plenty of room to grow and where it can remain for many years.

Plant comfrey seeds in almost any type of soil, and keep the area well watered until seedlings have established themselves. Thin plants to stand about 1 foot apart. Allow the plant to grow naturally for two or three years before you begin taking leaf cuttings. After several years, you can take cuttings at any time, from early spring through fall. In late fall, cut back the foliage once more and mulch.

Comfrey is a multi-purpose crop that yields continuously and requires very little care

Self-Seeding Vegetables

Self-seeding vegetables would seem to be the ultimate in care-free gardening, but that's not always the case. While crops like borage and dandelion are excellent vegetables that should be part of every gardener's plan, they can cause problems if grown in the bed or patch alongside annual vegetables. Seeding themselves year after year, they tend to expand their territory, often choking more delicate crops and literally taking over the garden. Plowing scatters their seeds over the entire area and creates a messy weeding job, if not an impossible one. Give these crops plenty of room to grow, preferably in their own permanent little patch. However, don't overlook them altogether. They are superior vegetables that will add much to your garden and table.

Borage is an odd, almost clumsy sort of plant that looks as though it belongs in a tropical jungle. Grown by the Romans as an herb to induce happiness and by the Elizabethans to bring courage, we now use it for the less grandiose purposes of making tea or as a delicious, cucumber-flavored green. Sow seeds in rich, light soil and mulch well after plants become established.

BORAGE AND DANDELION: *Borage (left) and dandelion are self-seeding vegetables that are best grown in their own permanent patch. Borage is excellent for making tea or used as cucumber-flavored greens, and dandelion makes an excellent spring salad green.*

Harvest leaves as soon as they are 3 to 5 inches long.

Mention planting dandelion to almost any gardener, and he will surely think you are crazy. Although many people are familiar with tasty dandelion salads and steamed spring greens, this plant in its wild form has become so pernicious a weed that virtually no one considers actually planting it; everyone is too busy weeding it out. However, a carefully tended, well-fertilized and weeded patch of an improved variety of dandelion is worth all the facetious remarks and bemused looks from your neighbors. Grown in loose, rich loam and picked young, these vegetables are the most wonderful of all spring greens. They are among the first plants to emerge from the frozen soil in late March or early April, making their slightly acid flavor and fresh, crisp texture particularly enjoyable. In addition, they are loaded with nutritional value.

Sow seeds ¼ to ½ inch deep in a fairly isolated patch. Plant in spring for an early summer crop, or plant in fall for a winter or early spring harvest. Thin early, setting plants about 4 inches apart in rows 1½ to 2 feet apart. Cuttings can be taken any time from the emergence of leaves in spring, until the leaves begin developing a slightly bitter flavor six weeks later, when the plants begin to bloom. At that time, dig up all plants and plant another crop.

Root Crops

All root and tuber crops require fairly light, porous soil rich in phosphorus. However, the Jerusalem artichoke, a sunflowerlike plant with a sweet, nutty tuber, and scorzonera, a black-skinned version of the slightly better-known oyster plant, are somewhat easier to raise than carrots, parsnips, potatoes or other typical root and tuber crops.

Jerusalem artichoke, also known as girasole or sunchoke, is usually propagated by tubers that you can purchase from several seedhouses across the country. As with potatoes, you can plant girasole tubers whole or in pieces, provided the pieces each have an eye from which stem tissue can grow. Plant tubers in late fall, around the time of the last expected fall frost. Soil should be well drained and neutral to slightly alkaline—that is, not very acid. Full sun is best. Place tubers 6 inches deep in rows about 3 feet apart, with 12 inches

Dandelion leaves are one of the richest vegetable sources of vitamin A, containing more than sweet potatoes, carrots or spinach

JERUSALEM ARTICHOKE AND SCORZONERA: *Jerusalem artichoke (left), with its sweet, nutty tuber and scorzonera, with its oyster-flavored roots, are easy-to-grow underground crops.*

PLANTING JERUSALEM ARTICHOKES: *In late fall, plant tubers 6 inches deep in rows about 3 feet apart, with 12 inches between each tuber in the rows.*

between each tuber in the rows. Water well during dry periods, and cover with a winter mulch. The following summer, support plants with stakes or trellises to encourage straight growth and prevent wind damage. Hill up the soil over the base of the plant so that tubers will be well protected from drying sun and wind. Plants grow 6 to 12 feet high and produce yellow blossoms in early fall. After the flowers have faded, the plants die down and the tubers can be dug.

Raised as a remedy for smallpox in the middle Ages, scorzonera was later a favorite vegetable of the Spanish, and it was also grown in eighteenth-century English and American kitchen gardens. In later years people found the dark color of the skin unpleasant, and the vegetable lost out to the bright hues of the carrot, parsnip and radish. However, since scorzonera is easy to grow and does not require soils as light as other root crops in order to develop straight, tender roots, it is well worth growing. It is a good companion plant to carrots since it is said to repel carrot flies.

Scorzonera has a delightful flavor, tolerates cold and will form straight roots in heavier soils where carrots or parsnips could be misshapen

Plant scorzonera seeds 1 inch deep in potassium-rich soil in early spring or late summer. Thin plants to stand about 4 inches apart in rows 15 inches apart. Harvest after a light frost or two, when the roots are long and slender, resembling a parsnip. Since plants are completely hardy, they may remain outdoors all winter long and be harvested in the dead of winter, provided a heavy mulch has kept the ground from freezing solid.

Legumes

Purple varieties of snap beans, various kinds of shell beans, broad beans, fava beans and soybeans are quickly becoming a part of many gardeners' yearly seed lists. In addition to these "unusuals," two other legumes worth trying are the asparagus pea and the oriental yard-long bean. The asparagus pea is a bush legume hardly resembling the ordinary garden pea. It grows just 1½ feet tall and has delicate light green leaves and reddish to purple pealike flowers. The pods are short, with four ribs or "wings" running longitudinally from top to bottom. They are said to taste like asparagus when eaten young.

Plant asparagus pea seeds in light, well-drained soil where plants will receive full sun. Sow only after all danger of frost has passed, spacing seeds 4 to 6 inches apart in 1-inch-deep furrows about 1 foot apart. You can also start seeds indoors for later transplanting to the garden.

ASPARAGUS PEA AND ASPARAGUS BEAN: *Aspar-agus pea (left), as the name implies, tastes like asparagus but the bushlike plants look nothing like ordinary peas. The asparagus bean, commonly called the yard-long bean, also has the character-istic taste of asparagus.*

The yard-long bean is a vegetable well known to aficionados of oriental cuisine. Although the long, thin beans are not usually a full 3 feet long, they will grow up to 2 feet in length and, like the winged bean, have a flavor resembling that of asparagus. Plant these bean seeds in spring after the ground has warmed and other vine crops are being planted. Since yard-long beans are climbers, you'll want to supply them with sturdy poles, trellises or other supports on which to climb. The plants are virtually pest-free, often resisting the very diseases and insects that damage other legumes.

Edible Pods

Okra, which is almost never available fresh in supermarkets throughout most of the United States, is one unusual vegetable that you must grow yourself if you want the experience of eating it. Strictly a warm-season vegetable, okra requires about eight weeks of temperatures continually above 60°F in order to reach maturity. For this reason, many gardeners must start seeds indoors in spring and later transplant to the garden. Okra needs a sunny site and rich, loamy soil. Plant seeds 1 inch apart

EDIBLE PODS: *Okra (left) and martynia are two very unusual crops that are worth growing for their pretty flowers and tasty seedpods.*

in rows about 2 feet apart, and later thin the plants to stand every foot. As plants develop, periodically treat them with weak manure tea for this crop is a fairly heavy feeder. Plants will grow anywhere from 3 to 10 feet tall, depending on the variety selected, and may require some staking for support. Harvest pods when they are about 3 inches long and still tender.

A lesser-known, pod-producing plant worthy of a place in your garden is martynia. Pods of this showy plant are sometimes found in dried flower arrangements, but they are also used in pickles and unusual soups. Native to the American Southwest, martynia is a 2-foot-high plant with large, soft leaves and pretty purple to yellow flowers. The edible seedpods resemble okra pods but have a long, curved beak that gives martynia the nickname "devil's claw."

Plant martynia seeds 1 inch deep and about 2 feet apart in a sunny, fertile location. Where the warm growing season is less than two months long, start seeds indoors and set plants outside about the time eggplant, tomatoes and peppers are transplanted. Although martynia plants require no staking, they may need some pruning or training to keep their heavy stems from encroaching on other garden plants. Harvest pods while still green and fuzzy for eating, or allow

Okra and martynia both produce beautiful flowers as well as edible pods

them to dry on the vine for interesting additions to flower arrangements.

Amaranth

The genus <u>Amaranthus</u> includes many different plants ranging from the common roadside pigweed and stately ornamentals to the edible types valued for their grain and leaves. Grain amaranth produces dramatic heads of small, white, protein-rich seeds. Because the process of cleaning these seeds is an involved and expensive one, grain amaranth is generally recommended for growing

AMARANTH: *Vegetable amaranth is a unique-flavored and nutritious substitute for spinach that is grown as a cut-and-come-again crop which will provide you with tasty greens all summer long.*

on a large, commercial scale. Of most interest to the home gardener is vegetable amaranth, which produces bountiful harvests of edible leaves all summer long. It is an excellent replacement for spinach since it is both heat-resistant and high yielding. It is also remarkably high in vitamins A and C, calcium, magnesium and iron.

Thanks to research efforts around the world, these ancient but forgotten food plants are being rediscovered by scientists, farmers and gardeners. Researchers from the Organic Gardening and Farming Research Center have traveled around the world to collect seeds of both grain and vegetable amaranths. At the research center, hundreds of amaranths are being cultivated and evaluated for their use as food crops in temperate climates. Since 1974, tests have been carried out at the grass roots level through a Reader Research Program. Over 13,000 Organic Gardening readers have planted seeds of three grain and three vegetable amaranths, recorded yields and noted other concerns related to cultivation. Their results confirm that the edible amaranths are unusually adaptable and efficient plants that deserve to be more widely grown.

Gardeners who wish to try vegetable amaranth will find several types offered by seed companies under the name tampala, Chinese spinach, hin choy and edible amaranth. Although the common names differ, almost all of these amaranths are the species A. tricolor or cultivars of that species. They are all upright, annual herbs that grow from 2 to 3 feet tall at maturity and bear wedge- or lance-shaped green leaves.

Vegetable amaranth requires a sunny, well-drained location to grow well. You can start seeds indoors for later transplanting, or sow the seeds right in the garden. Start seeds indoors in deep flats or individual peat pots about three weeks before setting out (about the time tomatoes are set out and beans are planted). The best transplants are 3 inches tall. Set seedlings 6 inches apart in all directions. Seeds can be sown outdoors when all danger of frost is past. Mix the tiny seeds with light soil or sand and scatter them evenly in rows 6 inches apart. Cover with 1/8 to 1/4 inch of soil, and keep the area moist until the seeds germinate one to two weeks later. Thin the plants to 6 inches apart when they are about 3 inches tall.

These plants are drought-resistant and can tolerate poor conditions, so mulch is needed only if the weather stays dry for a long period. Once the plants start growing and branching out, they create their own overlapping, leafy mulch.

Treat the vegetable amaranth as a cut-and-come-again crop, pinching off the leafy rosette at the top when each plant is 4 to 6 inches tall. Keep picking the tender rosettes at the ends of the branches as they reach usable size. The harvest can continue all summer until frost kills back the plants or short fall days cause the plants to bolt to seed. Use the leaves like spinach. Their distinctive flavor adds zest to familiar dishes.

For more information on growing amaranth and for a plethora of recipes, consult Amaranth: From the Past for the Future by John N. Cole (Emmaus, Pa. Rodale Press, 1979).

Cool-Season Crops

Standard cold-tolerant crops like broccoli, cabbage, endive, lettuce and spinach don't really produce substantial harvests in the very cool, dim environments of a growing frame or cloche. Such plants "hang on," but they grow very slowly and give relatively small yields for the amount of space they require. In the solar growing frame or tunnel cloche during spring, fall and winter, or even indoors in a cool room, they are significantly outproduced by a group of oriental vegetables that thrive in fluctuating temperatures and low light levels.

Rodale's researchers came across these crops while searching for high-yielding, hardy vegetables to raise in growing frames and cool greenhouses. They were looking for plants that would give lots of food in a short amount of time, would keep growing as temperatures hovered around the low- to mid-40s and would taste good enough to justify growing them. This search led them to scores of "new" crops, many of which are actually ancient staples of oriental cuisine. They found numerous greens for salads, quiches and crepes; crops for steaming and soup-making. Flavors range from a cabbagelike pungency to a mild, almost sweet taste.

Extend your season by growing high-yielding, cold-tolerant oriental vegetables in a cold frame, solar growing frame or cool greenhouse

A well-built growing frame planted with a range of these vegetables produces two to four 3-ounce servings of vegetables each day. When only the plants' outer leaves are harvested, most of the crops will continue to produce on a cut-and-come-again basis for weeks or even months. Not only will they thrive in the solar growing frame, but they may also be used to extend the outdoor growing season, may be raised in tunnel cloches where winter temperatures are slightly above freezing or may be grown indoors in a cool room where six hours of light can be guaranteed.

See the Cold-Tolerant Crops chart for a brief, descriptive list of some of the sturdy crops that have passed Rodale taste tests and have proved capable of thriving in temperatures that average about 40°F. Sources for all the plants mentioned in this chapter follow the Cold-Tolerant Crops chart in the separate listing of Seed Sources for Unusual and Cold-Tolerant Crops.

COLD-TOLERANT CROPS

Crop	Common Names	Days to Harvest	Description
Vegetables			
Brassica alboglabra	Chinese broccoli, Chinese kale, gai lohn	70	12–14 in. tall; dark-leaved, similar to Western broccoli; very high in vitamins and rich in flavor
Brassica campestris	Turnip, presto turnip, Tokyo turnip	30–50	12 in. tall; many varieties grow quickly; greens and roots edible; flavors range from mild to hot
Brassica chinensis	Pak choi, pak choy, spoon pak choi, purple pak choi, seppaku, flowering white cabbage, bok choy, mustard cabbage, celery cabbage	45–120	10–25 in. tall; leaves broad, loose and dark green, resembling chard; delicate, often sweet flavor
Brassica japonica	Mizuna, shui tsai, Chinese potherb mustard	45–50	Decorative, feathery plant; more tender than other brassicas; very mild cabbage flavor
Brassica juncea	Chinese mustard, purple mustard, Indian mustard, mustard spinach, gai choy	35–100	12–24 in. tall; deep ribbed leaves in a loose rosette; mild to hot peppery flavor
Brassica oleracea	Kale, flowering kale, dwarf kale, hwa choy	75–85	10–24 in. tall; dwarf varieties produce high yields, although slow-growing; mild flavor when leaves are young
Brassica pekinensis	Michihli, Chinese cabbage, pai tsai	50–100	8–25 in. tall; appearance and taste differ greatly from variety to variety
Chrysanthemum coronarium	Garland chrysanthemum	60 (to flowering)	24–48 in. tall; leaves have very strong, unusual flavor as they grow older; flowers brighten winter plantings

[continued on next page]

COLD-TOLERANT CROPS

Crop	Common Names	Days to Harvest	Description
Cichorium endivia	Endive	98	12 in. wide; flat rosette of wavy leaves; sharp flavor; excellent in salads
Cryptotaenia japonica	Mitsuba	60	Leaves similar to Italian parsley; celerylike flavor in seeds, leaves and stem; very hardy
Foeniculum vulgare	Sweet fennel	35–40	24 in. tall; feathery leaves with thick stem; anise flavor in seeds and leaves
Japanese greens	Hikoshima	70–105	9–24 in. tall; large group of many different species, most with attractive leafy rosettes; flavors range from cabbagelike to sweet and nutty
Lactuca sativa	Loose-heading lettuce	45–120	3–6 in. tall; attractive and tasty, but slow growing; wide range of flavors and textures
Lepidium sativum	Garden cress	20–30	8–10 in.; finely toothed leaves, long harvest period; pungent flavor
Nasturtium officinale	Watercress, sai yong choi	50	6–10 in. tall; does well in shade as long as soil is moist; small oval leaves have a refreshing peppery taste; useful in many dishes
Raphanus sativus	Chinese radish, winter radish, okhura, shogoin, lobok	60–100	12 in. tall; leaves and roots edible; very long harvest as cut-and-come-again greens

Crop	Common Names	Days to Harvest	Description
Spinacia oleracea	Spinach, Chinese spinach, hojo, Indian spinach, shueki, soshu	45–100	3–7 in. tall; varieties vary in taste and appearance; some grow flat while others are upright; taste may be salty and very mild or quite strong

Herbs

Crop	Common Names	Days to Harvest	Description
Anethum graveolens	Dill	35	Harvested young, when 4–6 in. tall; leaves add flavor to soups, vegetable dishes, sauerkraut and other dishes
Coriandrum sativum	Coriander	35	Harvest when 4–6 in. tall; dainty foliage with lacy flower heads; aromatic and flavorful in Mexican and oriental dishes
Origanum majorana	Sweet marjoram	70	8–10 in. tall; needs dry soil, but grows well in cool temperatures; flavorful leaves widely used in many dishes
Origanum vulgare	Oregano	70	6–8 in. tall; leaves on this bushy plant may be added to soups, salads, stews and sauces
Petroselinum crispum	Parsley, curled parsley	35	10–16 in. tall; prolific in cool weather; attractive foliage useful as seasoning and garnish
Satureja hortensis; S. montana	Summer savory, winter savory	65–75	12 in. tall; bushlike, woody plant; leaves small; whorls of tiny pink or white flowers; tangy flavor; useful in many dishes

SEED SOURCES FOR UNUSUAL AND COLD-TOLERANT CROPS

Note: Some companies charge for their catalogs, so inquire first if this is a concern for you.

Burgess Seed & Plant Co.
905 Four Seasons Rd.
Bloomington, IL 61701

W. Atlee Burpee Co.
300 Park Ave.
Warminster, PA 18974

Casa Yerba
Star Route 2, Box 21
Days Creek, OR 97429

Comstock, Ferre & Co.
263 Main St.
Wethersfield, CT 06109

William Dam Seeds
Highway 8
West Flamboro, Ontario
Canada L0R 2K0

De Giorgi Co., Inc.
P.O. Box 413
Council Bluffs, IA 51502

J. A. Demonchaux Co., Inc.
827 N. Kansas Ave.
Topeka, KS 66608

Ferndale Gardens
Order Processing Center
710 Nursery La.
Canoga Park, CA 91303

Henry Field Seed & Nursery Co.
407 Sycamore St.
Shenandoah, IA 51602

Grace's Gardens
10 Bay St.
Westport, CT 06880

Gurney Seed & Nursery Co.
1917 Page St.
Yankton, SD 57079

Joseph Harris Co., Inc.
Moreton Farm
Rochester, NY 14624

Hemlock Hill Herb Farm
Hemlock Hill Road, Box 415
Litchfield, CT 06759
(perennial and biennial herb
    plants only)

Herbst Brothers Seedsmen, Inc.
1000 N. Main St.
Brewster, NY 10509

J. L. Hudson, Seedsman
A World Seed Service
P.O. Box 1058
Redwood City, CA 94064

Johnny's Selected Seeds
Albion, ME 04910

Kitazawa Seed Co.
356 W. Taylor St.
San Jose, CA 95110

Le Jardin du Gourmet
West Danville, VT 05873

Meadowbrook Herbs & Things
Whispering Pine Road
Wyoming, RI 02898

Nichols Garden Nursery
1190 N. Pacific Highway
Albany, OR 97321

Geo. W. Park Seed Co., Inc.
Box 31
Greenwood, SC 29647

Redwood City Seed Co.
P.O. Box 361
Redwood City, CA 94064

Otto Richter & Sons
Box 26
Goodwood, Ontario
Canada L0C 1A0

Seedway, Inc.
Box 1817
Hall, NY 14463

R. H. Shumway Seedsman, Inc.
Rockford, IL 61101

Stokes Seeds, Inc.
737 Main St., Box 548
Buffalo, NY 14240

Sunrise Enterprises
P.O. Box 10058
Elmwood, CT 06110

Thompson & Morgan, Inc.
P.O. Box 100
Farmingdale, NJ 07727

Tsang and Ma International
1306 Old Country Road
Belmont, CA 94002

Vermont Bean Seed Co.
Garden Lane
Bomoseen, VT 05732

Well-Sweep Herb Farm
317 Mt. Bethel Rd.
Port Murray, NJ 07865

Dr. Yoo Farm
P.O. Box 290
College Park, MD 20740

DESIGNING GARDEN EXPERIMENTS

T he longer most gardeners grow vegetables, the more they appreciate just how complex a task it is. Every year, they become more aware of the variables — rainfall, soil, seeds, insects and any number of other factors seem to have more control than they do over the health and productivity of the crops. Why did that early carrot crop fail? Why did one variety of cucumber do so much better than the other? Was it the weather? Was it the seed? What about the planting date or that new mulching material?

You can answer most of these questions through simple, systematic investigation. It's the best way to get to know your own garden. With a few controlled experiments, you can determine which techniques will maximize your garden's production, which varieties are better than others for your garden and which materials are really worth using. It is possible to test the effectiveness of various fertilizers, to compare the benefits of deep and shallow digging or to search out beneficial planting companions.

Conditions in each garden are unique, and experimentation is still the best way to find the most effective methods for your particular situation

Such projects aren't for all gardeners. They take time and energy, but they can be fun, too. If you're a seasoned gardener who's serious about making your plot of ground produce healthier, more productive crops, then you'll find rewards for your labors. One or two experiments can take the guesswork out of certain aspects of gardening — and save lots of time and energy in the long run.

The scientific method is a complex subject, particularly as it applies to work in the home garden. This brief introduction may entice you to further study. For more information on experimental techniques and analysis, read Improve Your Gardening with Backyard Research by Lois Levitan (Emmaus, Pa.: Rodale Press, 1980).

Planning the Experiment

Begin by choosing a problem you'd like to investigate. Your experiment can be fairly simple, such as a straightforward yield comparison of two crop varieties, two mulching materials or two companion planting arrangements. A more complex experiment might examine several different variables, such as the responses of corn, beans and squash to mulches of salt hay, plastic film and newspaper. The more variables you intend to study, the more room you'll need to lay out plots and permit replication. Experiments involving just two or three plots are much simpler to manage in the home garden.

State your hypothesis in such a way that it can be proven true or false by the experiment. This will force you to narrow your subject, and it will really determine just what you hope to find out. For instance, your hypothesis might read, "Given the same growing conditions in my garden, variety A will produce more cucumbers than variety B." Another example: "Melons mulched with black plastic will produce fruit earlier than those mulched with 6 inches of lawn clippings and given equal treatment in my garden." Each of these hypotheses presents a clear problem that can seemingly be answered by setting up two plots and comparing the results. Variety A will or will not outproduce variety B; black plastic will or will not induce early fruiting in melons.

Such experiments would be quite simple to run in a laboratory setting, but they become much more complex in the garden, where there are numerous uncontrollable varieties. Care must be taken to understand these natural variables and to design the experiment so that their effects are minimized. This is the challenge of horticultural experimentation.

Weather changes from year to year, often drastically. If variety A will outproduce variety B this year, during a drought, how can you be sure it will do the same next

To design a successful experiment, the hypothesis you wish to test should be a statement that will be proven either true or false by the results of the trial

year when rainfall is normal? Black plastic may produce earlier fruit when temperatures are below normal, but how will it compare with lawn clippings when temperatures are normal or above normal? These questions can't be answered with just one experiment in just one season. To have any certainty about a given result of almost any experiment, you must repeat the test for several years, keeping careful records of minimum and maximum daily temperatures, rainfall and other conditions for each year. In this way, you can overcome the effects of varying weather conditions. By comparing results obtained in several years, you will find evidence of the success or failure of the treatment you are testing.

Soil quality is another variable that you can't control; you can, however, manage it. Soil in even the smallest garden consists of many different textures and minerals. One corner of the garden may be a slightly alkaline patch of clay, while another corner is a neutral loam. A spring might bubble up in one section, while another area is much drier. To overcome these variations, you may wish to have your soil tested in several different areas. Contact your state agricultural extension service for some soil-testing kits. Decide where you would like to establish the experimental plots and take a representative sample from each one. Comparison of the test results will help you determine which plots are sufficiently uniform for the experiment.

It is also possible to shape and lay out the plots so that variations in soil, sunlight or wind are shared equally by each section. For example, if your test area is on a slope, divide it into plots running from top to bottom. This design will minimize the effects of the slope and allow for the fact that more fertile soil may lie at the bottom of the hill.

Where there are no obvious differences in conditions, lay out the plots randomly. If many variables are involved and many plots are required, randomization becomes a complex mathematical problem requiring the use of special randomization tables and some calculations. You can find this information in books on statistics and the scientific method. Lois Levitan's book, mentioned earlier in this chapter, is another source.

When only two or three variables are being examined, randomizing is fairly simple. Just divide the experimental

Lay out the trial plots where soil quality is more uniform and in such a way that the plots are equally affected by other variable conditions of the site

area into two sections and divide each section in half. For instance, flip a coin to decide which of two varieties will go in the first half of a section. The comparison variety will be run in the remaining half. Flip again to decide which treatment will be in the first half of section two. The comparison treatment will go in the remaining half. In this way you have at least begun to minimize differences and spread them across all four plots.

An even better way to lay out plots, particularly if you have four to eight variables, is the Latin Square design. The experimental area is marked off in a grid pattern, and the treatments are arranged in rotation down each row. The result for an experiment with four variables would look like this:

a	b	c	d
b	c	d	a
c	d	a	b
d	a	b	c

Thus, the plot in the upper left corner receives treatment a, the one next to it treatment b, and so forth across the experimental area. Each treatment is replicated four times in four different areas of the garden.

Whenever treatments are being compared, such as different mulches or organic fertilizers or sprays, always include one control plot in which no treatment is applied. If you wish to test the effectiveness of a garlic spray and a hot pepper spray against Mexican bean beetles, treat one plot with garlic, one with the hot pepper and one with nothing, and replicate each two or three times across the experimental area.

Locate your experimental plots well within the established garden area, not out in the corner of a back lot or in a poorer section of the cultivated garden. Make treatment areas wide enough to allow for the border effect, which will cause outer plants to respond differently from those well within the plot. Carefully mark off the growing areas with string or rope, and label each using a plastic label and grease pencil.

Keeping Records

Careful records are essential for valid experimentation and meaningful analysis of results. Start a field book in which you write your hypothesis, illustrate your plot layout and record your data.

To observe the results of the trial and collect data, it will be necessary to take representative samples and to devise specific criteria for sampling procedures. For example, select a manageable number of "sample" plants that are well within the experimental plot, and count the insects on five of their leaves. Or, select a few more plants from each plot, and describe their damage in terms of degree and assign a value. For example, 60 percent leaf loss or more might be given a rating of 5; 50 percent leaf loss = 4; 25-40 percent leaf loss = 3; 10-25 percent leaf loss = 2; 5-10 percent leaf loss = 1; less than 5 percent leaf loss = 0.

Analyzing the Data

Begin by listing the data you've collected from each plot. This might be a measure of yield, height, weight or any other factors you have quantified. Convert these numbers to graph form, where possible, so that you can visually determine the difference between your treatments. To make your results really meaningful, you'll need to analyze them statistically, using some pretty hefty calculations such as the mean range of values and the standard deviation. You'll want to test for the significant different between treatments, to know whether the change you noted between treatments one and two was meaningful or simply a sign of chance at play. Consult a reliable book on statistical information for these formulas. Or, look closely at your graphs and numbers and be content with a bit of common sense at this point.

Analysis of results can be the most complex aspect of your entire experiment and may lead you to wish you'd planned the tests more carefully

SAVING YOUR OWN SEEDS

R aising garden seeds may seem too involved for the home gardener, but it's really not half as complicated as professional seed growers would like us to think. After all, plants in woods and fields produce seed without our help. Even many garden crops — tomatoes and potatoes, for example — volunteer their offspring which often turn out to be more vigorous and tasty than our purchased crops. In order to produce first-rate seeds consistently, all we need to do is follow nature's ways and learn to be selective in the crops we choose as parents.

Saving your own vegetable seeds means saving a lot of money and putting yourself in control of just how much your garden costs each year. But, even more important, it can mean saving varieties that have adapted to your specific area — even preserving special heirloom vegetables that are not widely marketed.

Flowering, seed-producing crops may be classified in this way: annuals, which bloom and mature, produce seeds and die in the same year; biennials, which go to seed in the second year of growth; and perennials, which live and bear seed year after year. Most vegetables are annual or biennial. Asparagus and rhubarb are the only widely grown perennial vegetables, and they are seldom propagated from seed. Among the many annuals are beans, broccoli, corn, lettuce, onions and tomatoes. Biennials include most root crops, brussels sprouts, cabbage, cauliflower and celery.

Self-Pollinating and Cross-Pollinating Species
Within each of these categories are both self-pollinating and cross-pollinating species. In self-pollinating species, like tomatoes, beans and peas, pollination takes place within each flower, and no pollen is transferred from

Homegrown seeds are fun to produce and much more reliable than you may think plant to plant. Since there is usually no genetic input from other plants, their seeds produce crops exactly like the parent crop. Successive generations will continue to breed true to type unless flowers are deliberately fertilized with pollen from another plant.

Cross-pollinating species do not naturally breed true to type. Since insects or wind carry pollen from one flower to another, genetic traits from many different plants are constantly being scrambled together. Seeds from cabbages, carrots, corn, cucumbers, melons, squash and scores of other cross-pollinators will not produce plants that resemble the parent crop. Within the same species, and sometimes just the same genus, many different varieties may interbreed. It all depends on what is growing nearby. A salad-type cucumber may be crossed with a pickling type in the next row, butternut squash may cross with zucchini, or beets with Swiss chard. Although seeds from such plants may look perfectly "normal," they will not produce offspring quite like the parent plant. Occasionally this random cross results in a great new variety, but successive generations will not be uniform.

For seed production, potential cross-pollinators must be isolated from one another. This includes not only similar varieties and cultivars of the same species but related weeds as well. Commercial growers separate varieties by several thousand feet; in the home garden, 200 feet is adequate for most crops, and 1,000 feet will almost always assure a pure strain.

Make sure the seeds you save are from nonhybrid varieties. Seeds from plants of the first hybrid generation will not produce duplicates of the parent plant

Begin your seed growing with a few favorite nonhybrid varieties. Hybrid plants of the first (F-1) generation should not be used because they don't breed true. They are the result of a cross of two genetically different parent plants, creating a first generation that is more vigorous, uniform and productive than either of the parents. The second generation will have none of these qualities. Well-established, time-tested nonhybrids are needed for standard seed production. Annual, self-pollinating types are easiest to handle, but don't be scared off by biennial and cross-pollinating vegetables. With only a little care and thought, these two will bring successful results.

Plant your garden just as you would every year, taking care to separate any cross-pollinators you are going to preserve. Keep very careful records on each potential parent plant so you can objectively judge its performance and choose the best one for next year's seeds. Write down the dates you sow seed, the rate of germination, notes on insect and disease resistance, all-around vigor, earliness, tolerance of heat or cold, taste and any other characteristics you find desirable in that particular vegetable. As you find individual plants that have these qualities, mark them with a bit of string and closely follow their progress to maturity.

Just one parent plant is needed to provide seeds for self-pollinating species, but choose several parents when the crop is a cross-pollinator. This will maintain a broad genetic base and keep the strain vigorous and productive. Exceptions to this rule are the several varieties of squash, which can be inbred for generations without showing any deterioration.

By the end of the growing season, you will have decided which plants will be next year's parents, and you can collect seeds from flowering and fruiting annuals. Timing and methods of seed collection differ greatly from crop to crop. In some instances, seeds are left to dry on the plant before you collect them; in other cases, they must be harvested sooner. Check the Seed Production and Harvest chart on the next page for specific guidelines for a number of crops.

SEED PRODUCTION AND HARVEST

The abbreviations used in the left column are as follows: A indicates an annual crop; B indicates a biennial; C stands for cross-pollinating; S means the crop is self-pollinating.

Crop	Method
Beans (A, S)	Uproot bush beans after leaves have fallen and pods have browned. Let pole beans dry completely on the vines; shell pods when they are crispy dry.
Beets and Swiss Chard (B, C)	First year: Sow seeds several months before heavy fall frosts. Raise just one variety of beet or chard each year to avoid crossing problems. Harvest roots before heavy frost. Trim tops down to 1 in. and store roots in moist soil at 40°F.
	Second year: In early spring, plant roots just under soil. Harvest seeds when dry and brown by uprooting plants and curing in a dry place until completely dry.
Broccoli (A, C)	Allow 200 ft. or more between varieties of this crop or brussels sprouts, cabbage, cauliflower, kale and kohlrabi in bloom. Sow early. Allow choice heads to produce seed; harvest when pods are brittle.
Brussels Sprouts and Cabbage (B, C)	Allow 200 ft. between broccoli, brussels sprouts, cabbage, cauliflower, kale and kohlrabi.
	First year: Uproot best plants when at peak for eating. Cut off top growth and bury root in moist sand; store at near freezing temperatures.
	Second year: Replant in spring; stake plants to support tall seedstalks. Cut plants when most pods are brown; let dry on canvas in the sun before threshing.
Carrots (B, C)	First year: Allow 200 ft. between varieties, and keep Queen Anne's Lace well mowed to prevent its flowering and possible crosses. Seed in early to midsummer; mulch heavily at end of season.
	Second year: Harvest seeds when they have turned brown.
Corn (A, C)	Allow 200 ft. for a decent crop; 1,000 ft. for a purer strain. Harvest ears 3 to 5 weeks after eating stage, when husks are brown; dry further by hanging in an airy place.
Cucumbers (A, C)	Allow 200 ft. between cucumber varieties. Harvest fruits when pickling varieties are golden and table varieties are white. Slice fruit in half vertically; remove seeds and put them in a warm place. After fermentation (about 3 to 6 days) viable seed will sink to bottom of container and will feel rough to the touch; wash best seeds several times and dry on screens.

Crop	Method
Eggplant (A, S)	Harvest seeds when fruits are at peak for eating; remove pulp and seeds and wash clean. Dry completely before storing.
Lettuce (A, S)	Sow early in spring to assure flowering the same season. Harvest by cutting plants when half the flowers have gone to seed. Allow to dry on a canvas, and shake off seeds.
Muskmelons (A, C)	Allow 200 ft. between varieties of melon. Pick melon when at peak ripeness; scoop out seeds and pulp and let ferment at room temperature for several days, stirring occasionally. When a thin liquid has formed around each seed, fermentation is complete, and good seeds can be removed from the bottom of the container. Wash thoroughly, and dry on paper or screens.
Peas (A, S)	Cross-pollination sometimes occurs, so it's best to separate varieties by 100 ft. or to intercrop with a tall vegetable. Leave pods on the vine until they are brittle; uproot plants, and cure them in a dry area. When brittle, open pods and remove seeds.
Peppers (A, S)	Harvest best fruits when fully ripe, usually red or yellow. Remove the mass of seeds and allow them to dry, then shake off seeds.
Spinach (A, C)	Plant just one variety to keep strain pure. Sow seed in early spring or in fall if winters are warm. Remove stunted plants and those that bolt quite early from the row. Cut good plants when seeds have ripened and plant has turned completely brown; allow to cure in a protected place. When dry, shake off seeds, rubbing to clean debris.
Squash and Pumpkins (A, C)	Separate varieties of same species by 100 or more ft. Harvest when fruits are completely mature and well past edible stage (usually about 2 months after peak). Wash seeds and select the plump, firm ones that remain on the bottom of the bucket. Dry on screens.
Tomatoes (A, S)	Harvest best fruit when at peak ripeness; crush in a container and allow to ferment at 70°F for several days, stirring occasionally. After thin liquid develops, fermentation is complete; wash seed thoroughly, and dry on screens in the sun.
Watermelons (A, C)	Separate varieties by at least 200 ft. Harvest when melons are at peak stage for eating; wash in water and save only the heaviest, plumpest seeds. Dry seeds thoroughly before storage.

Biennials need special treatment. In very warm areas of the South and the West Coast, some biennial crops may be left in the ground all winter and will set seed early in spring. However, in most of North America, tender and half-hardy biennials must be uprooted in fall, buried in sand, soil and peat and stored in a cool, damp cellar for the winter. In spring, cut away deteriorated leaves and stems, and replant. When the plant goes to seed that summer, you can collect seeds for the next generation.

Storing Seeds

Before storing seeds, wash, disinfect and dry them thoroughly. Wash the seeds from melons, tomatoes, peppers, squash as well as other "wet" seeds as you remove them from their fruits. Dry seeds, such as bean and pea seeds, may be simply threshed and shaken over a screen to sift out any lightweight plant debris. To disinfect seeds and protect them from bacterial and fungal diseases, soak them in a solution of one part liquid household chlorine bleach to ten parts water for 5 to 15 minutes. Rinse them in running water for 5 more minutes, and dry well. Place the seeds on a screen, and

DRYING SEEDS: *After washing and disinfecting, dry seeds for storage on a screen suspended over a box that contains a 25-watt light bulb.*

set them in a warm, dry spot, but not in direct sunlight. For really dry seeds—and much better storage success—suspend seed screens over a box with a 25-watt bulb, or set them in the oven with the pilot light on. Don't let the temperature rise above 95°F, or you will diminish their viability.

When the seeds are good and dry, they are ready for storage. Because heat and humidity are the worst enemies of vegetable seeds, storage places must be cool and dry. As a general rule, the temperature in degrees Fahrenheit plus the relative humidity of the storage place should add up to less than 100. Thus, when the temperature is 55°F, the relative humidity must be less than 45 percent in order to maintain good seed storage conditions. If the temperature drops, a higher humidity would be tolerable.

Bean and pea seeds prefer air circulation during storage and should be placed in envelopes for storage. Most other seeds need airtight containers such as sealed jars, cans or plastic bags. A tiny cloth bag filled with dry milk or silica gel and placed in each jar will help absorb excess moisture. If the container is truly air- and moistureproof, if may be placed in the refrigerator, where seeds will maintain a high germination rate for several years. Label containers with varietal names, dates and lot numbers.

Before planting in spring, test any stored seed to determine its germination rate. To do this, count out 25, 50 or 100 seeds and spread them evenly on a dampened paper towel or cotton blotter. If you wish to be really precise, you may draw a grid on the blotter and place one seed in each spot. Next, place another damp piece of blotter over the seeds and carefully roll the pieces up tightly and fasten with a rubber band. Set the roll upright and leave at room temperature. Sprinkle it with water whenever it becomes dry. After the suggested "days to germination" for that type of seed, unroll the cloth and count the number of seeds that have sprouted. This may be converted to a percentage that represents your germination rate. This number will help you know just how thickly to plant seed in the garden.

Preserving Old Varieties
Ever wonder what happened to the Jacob's cattle bean? How about the violet radish, Aberdeen cabbage

Unless we continue to propagate and preserve old seeds, the sweet corn which the Indians gave the pilgrims, the hotspur peas and Portugal onions which Washington and Jefferson grew and a host of other vegetables passed on for generations will become extinct

and the good old mangelwurzel? Old favorites like these aren't easy to find nowadays. Most seed companies are too interested in developing new hybrids — square tomatoes, supersonic sweet corn and cosmic cucumbers — that they don't keep track of such quiet old-timers. Yet, it seems a shame to ignore them. These varieties represent a heritage that is in danger of being lost forever.

If they disappear, we lose not only a taste of our past but the hope of our future. Every year 100-200 plants become extinct. The myriad native food plants we once cultivated and harvested have been abandoned in favor of a few hybrid supercrops. Their loss means that fewer kinds of plants are being used to feed the world's people. As the genetic base is narrowed, the possibility of massive crop losses from disease and insect infestations increases. If new genetic material from different plants is not available, then new resistant varieties cannot be bred.

Scientists around the world are aware of this problem and have established seed banks where endangered species and varieties are stored. The U.S. seed bank has over 100,000 seed varieties in storage. But the most exciting seed saving is happening at a grass roots level. Gardeners across the country and around the world are not just storing heirloom seeds but are growing them as well. Motivated by a desire to understand the past and to preserve genetic material for the future, these gardeners are trying to locate old, "lost" varieties, raise them and save much of their seed from year to year. Then, through the Seed Savers Exchange, a 400-member organization started in 1974, they trade their seeds, thereby spreading the varieties across the country and preserving them from extinction.

Gardeners who wish to search out and preserve traditional varieties should begin by collecting varieties of a single crop. Find out what types are grown locally and grow them all, being sure to maintain purity in the strains. Look through seed catalogs from some of the smaller suppliers, for many of them offer a good selection of old standbys. Talk to elderly gardeners to see what they plant; often the older varieties are still being saved, and gardeners are eager to share their seeds. Searches through local history books, old letters and seed catalogs published in the last century can turn up names of other varieties no longer available from the major companies but possibly still growing in someone's backyard.

If you're serious about raising heirloom vegetables and want to share your varieties with other gardeners, consider joining the Seed Savers Exchange. The $3 membership fee will put you in contact with other gardeners and with lots of information on plant histories and seed storage techniques. The organization publishes an annual catalog that lists its members, the seeds they have saved and those they'd like to acquire. It also runs a small seed bank that preserves seeds of beans and other crops and increases the reserves. Although not for gardeners who just want to expand their personal collection of garden seeds, the Exchange is perfect for those truly committed to sharing their knowledge and their seeds. For more information, send a stamped, self-addressed envelope to the founder, Kent Whealy, RFD 2, Box 92, Princeton, MO 64673.

SEED SOURCES FOR OLD VARIETIES

Note: Some companies charge for their catalogs, so inquire first if this is a concern for you.

Abundant Life Seed Foundation
P.O. Box 772
Port Townsend, WA 98368

Comstock, Ferre & Co.
263 Main St.
Wethersfield, CT 06109

De Giorgi Co., Inc.
P.O. Box 413
Council Bluffs, IA 51502

Charles C. Hart Seed Co.
304 Main St.
Wethersfield, CT 06109

Hemlock Hill Herb Farm
Hemlock Hill Road
Litchfield, CT 06759

Herbst Brothers Seedsmen, Inc.
1000 N. Main St.
Brewster, NY 10509

J. L. Hudson, Seedsman
A World Seed Service
P.O. Box 1058
Redwood City, CA 94064

Johnny's Selected Seeds
Albion, ME 04910

L. L. Olds Seed Co.
P.O. Box 7790
Madison, WI 53707

Nichols Garden Nursery
1190 N. Pacific Highway
Albany, OR 97321

[continued on next page]

SEED SOURCES FOR OLD VARIETIES

Redwood City Seed Co.
P.O. Box 361
Redwood City, CA 94064

R. H. Shumway Seedsman, Inc.
Rockford, IL 61101

Stokes Seeds, Inc.
737 Main St., Box 548
Buffalo, NY 14240

Vermont Bean Seed Co.
Garden Lane
Bomoseen, VT 05732

BIBLIOGRAPHY

All of these books provide helpful information for advanced gardeners.

Aquatias, A. Intensive Culture of Vegetables. Harrisville, N.H.: Solar Survival Press, 1978.

Bartholomew, Mel. Square Foot Gardening. Emmaus, Pa.: Rodale Press, 1981.

Bubel, Nancy. The Seed-Starter's Handbook. Emmaus, Pa.: Rodale Press, 1978.

Cole, John N. Amaranth: From the Past for the Future. Emmaus, Pa.: Rodale Press, 1979.

Cuthbertson, Tom. Alan Chadwick's Enchanted Garden. New York: E. P. Dutton, 1978.

Editors of Organic Gardening magazine. Getting the Most from Your Garden. Emmaus, Pa.: Rodale Press, 1980.

Flawn, Louis N. Gardening with Cloches. Rev. ed. London: Gifford, 1967.

Hills, Lawrence D. Fertility Gardening. London: Henry Doubleday Research Association, 1980.

_____. Save Your Own Seed. Essex, England: Henry Doubleday Research Association, 1975.

Johnston, Robert, Jr. Growing Garden Seeds. Albion, Me.: Johnny's Selected Seeds, 1976.

Langham, Derald G. Circle Gardening. Old Greenwich, Conn.: Devin-Adair Co., 1978.

Larkcom, Joy. Vegetables from Small Gardens. London: Faber & Faber, 1976.

Levitan, Lois. Improve Your Gardening with Backyard Research. Emmaus, Pa.: Rodale Press, 1980.

Men's Gardening Clubs of America. A to Z Hints for the Vegetable Gardener. Charlotte, Vt.: Garden Way Publishing Co., 1977.

Miller, Douglas. Vegetable and Herb Seed Growing for the Gardener and Small Farmers. Hersey, Mich.: Bullkill Creek Publishing Co., 1977.

Philbrick, Helen, and Gregg, Richard B. Companion Plants. Rev. ed. Old Greenwich, Conn.: Devin-Adair Co., 1966.

Powell, Thomas and Powell, Betty. The Avant Gardener. Boston: Houghton Mifflin Co., 1975.

Riotte, Louise. Secrets of Companion Planting for Successful Gardening. Charlotte, Vt.: Garden Way Publishing Co., 1975.

Seymour, John. The Self-Sufficient Gardener. Garden City, N.Y.: Doubleday & Co., 1979.

Thompson, Homer C., and Kelly, William C. Vegetable Crops. 5th ed. New York: McGraw-Hill Book Co., 1957.

Wolf, Ray, ed. Solar Growing Frame. Emmaus, Pa.: Rodale Press, 1980.

INDEX

A
Alfalfa, as fertilizer, **65–66**
Amaranth, growing of, **112–14**
Aphid
 bean, **74**
 pea, **74**

B
Bamboo structures, for plant support, **56–58**
Band planting, **43–44**
Barrier, rodent
 other plants as, **49**
 vertical screen as, **14–15**
Base temperature, for vegetable crops, **28**
Bean aphid, **74**
Beetle
 asparagus, **75**

Colorado potato, **75**
cucumber
 spotted, **78**
 striped, **79**
 Japanese, **76**
 Mexican bean, **77**
 striped flea, **75**
Block planting, **43**
 square-foot technique and, **47–48**
Borage, growing of, **106–7**
Border planting, **43–44**

C
Cabbage looper, **80**
Cages, wire-mesh, for plant support, **54–56**
Circle planting, **48–50**
Cloches, **24, 92–97**
 A-frame, **96**
 as frost protection, **92–93**

tunnel, **96–97**
Comfrey
  growing of, **105**
  medicinal value of, **105**
Compaction, of soil
  alternatives for, **5–15**
  reduction of crop efficiency and, **4–5**
Companion planting, **35**
  flowers for, **42**
  herbs for, **42**
Compost, as liquid fertilizer, **67**
Cool-season crops, **114–17**
Corn earworm, **76**
Corn rootworm, northern, **78**
Crops
  cool season, **114–17**
    seed sources for, **118–19**
  short-season, succession planting and, **27**
  vegetable
    base temperature for, **28**
    interplanting and, **29–30**
    relay planting and, **23–26**
    succession planting and, **22–27**

D
Dandelion, growing of, **107**
Degree-days, timing harvest for, **27–29**
Double-digging, growing beds and, **6–13**
Double-row planting, improving yields and, **44–46**

F
Fertilizer, organic
  alfalfa as, **65–66**
  recipes for, **66–69**
  in solar growing frames, **91**
Flat-topped bed, **12–13**
Flies, parasitic, as insect predator, **84**
Flowers, companion planting and, **42**
Foliar sprays, **68–69**
Frost, protection from, **92–93**

G
Garden
  experiments for, **120–24**
  planning of, **21–22**
Gardening
  record-keeping and, **124**

various methods of, **15–20**
Growing beds, **5–7, 36–37**
  between-plant spacing and, **38**
    equidistant, **40**
    square-center, **40**
  double-digging for, **6–13**
  types of, **12–15, 37–43**
Gypsy moth, **77**

H
Harvesting
  degree-days for timing of, **27–29**
  of seeds, **128–29**
  staggering of, **22**
Heat units, **28–29**
Herbs, companion planting and, **42**
Hybrid plants, **126–27**

I
Insect control
  companion planting and, **35**
  interplanting and, **87**
Insect predators, **81–84**
Insects, emergence time of, **73–80**
Interplanting
  insect control and, **87**
  light needs of, **32–33**
  nutrient needs and, **33–35**
  rowed beds and, **39–43**
  vegetable crops and, **29–30**

J
Japanese beetle, **76**
Jerusalem artichoke, growing of, **107–9**

L
Lacewings, green, as insect predator, **83**
Ladybugs, as insect predator, **82–83**
Legumes, growing of, **109–10**
Light needs, interplanting and, **32–33**

M
Manure tea, as liquid fertilizer, **67–68**
Mexican bean beetle, **77**
Mounded design beds, **12–13**
Mulch, plastic, **97–98**

N

No-till garden, **17–20**
Nutrient needs, interplanting and, **33–35**

O

Organic mulch, alfalfa as, **65–66**

P

Pan gardening, construction of, **15–16**
Pea aphid, **74**
Pelletizing, seeds and, **80–81**
Pest control, natural, **72–87**
 insect predators and, **81–84**
 interplanting and, **87**
 pelletizing seeds for, **80–81**
 sprays for, **84–87**
Planting
 band or border, **43–44**
 block, **43**
 companion, **35, 42**
 intensive, **35**
 interplanting, **29–30**
 relay, **23–29**
 succession, **22–29**
Plants
 light needs of, **32–33**
 nutrient needs of, **33–35**
 shapes and sizes of, **30–32**
Plant support
 bamboo structures for, **56–58**
 trellises for, **59–64**
 wire-mesh cages for, **54–56**
Plastic, black
 as mulch, **98**
 for week growth reduction, **18**
Praying mantids, as insect predator, **83**
Pruning, vertical gardening and, **52–53**
Pyramid trellis, building of, **60–61**

R

Record-keeping, gardening and, **124**
Relay planting, **23–26**
Reservoirs, **69–71**
 feeding plants from, **69**
Rodent barrier, vertical screen as, **14–15**
Root crops, **107–9**
Rowed beds, **37–43**
 interplanting and, **39–43**

S

Screen, vertical, as rodent barrier, **14–15**
Sea kale, growing of, **104–5**

Seed(s)
 cross-pollinating of, **125–27**
 harvesting of, **128–29**
 old varieties of
  preserving of, **131–33**
  sources for, **133–34**
 production of, **128–29**
 raising your own, **125**
 self-pollinating, **125–26**
 storage of, **130–31**
Seed sources, cold-tolerant crops and, **118–19**
Sod, removal of, **8–9**
Soil, **4–5**
 improvement of, **25**
Solar growing frames, **88–92**
Sprays, natural, as pest control, **84–87**
Squash bug, **79**
Squash vine border, **79**
String trellis, building of, **64**
Strip-cropping, **46–47**
Succession planting, **22–27**
 short-season crops and, **27**
 to discourage pests, **25**

T

Tepee trellis, building of, **59–60**
Tomato hornworm, **77**
Trellises
 for plant support, **58–59**
 types of, **59–64**
Trenching, **15–17**
Turf loam, making of, **9**
Two-dimensional trellis, building of, **61–63**

V

Vegetables
 root, **107–9**
 self-seeding, **106–7**
 unusual, **102–14**
Vertical gardening, **51–64**

W

Wasps, parasitic, as insect predator, **84**
Weed growth, reduction of, **18**
Windbreaks
 fences as, **98–99**
 natural, **99–100**

Y

Yield, improving of, **44–45**